THE SCHOOL MEDIATOR'S FIELD GUIDE

THE SCHOOL MEDIATOR'S FIELD GUIDE

Prejudice

Sexual Harassment

Large Groups

And Other Daily Challenges

RICHARD COHEN

School Mediation Associates

Watertown, Massachusetts

The School Mediator's Field Guide
Prejudice, Sexual Harassment, Large Groups and Other Daily Challenges

By Richard Cohen

Published by
School Mediation Associates
134-B Standish Road, Watertown, MA 02472 USA
617-926-5969
smabooks@schoolmediation.com
www.schoolmediation.com

First Printing May 1999
10 9 8 7 6 5 4 3 2 1

Printed in the United States of America

ISBN: 0-9664408-0-3
Library of Congress Catalog Card Number: 98-90358

WE MAY BE ANGRY AND FIGHT,
WE MAY FEEL KINDLY AND WANT
PEACE...IT IS ABOUT THE SAME.
THE WORLD WILL BE REGENERATED
BY THE PEOPLE WHO RISE
ABOVE THESE PASSIVE WAYS AND
HEROICALLY SEEK, BY WHATEVER
HARDSHIP, BY WHATEVER TOIL,
THE METHODS BY WHICH PEOPLE
CAN AGREE.

MARY PARKER FOLLET

For Rachel (always)

Acknowledgments

Thank you first to the colleagues and friends who co-authored chapters: Denise Messina (sexual harassment), Bernadette Murphy (sexual orientation harassment), and Melissa Brodrick (student-parent). It was a pleasure working with each of you.

There is no single "expert" on mediating all of the conflicts discussed in this book. To be most useful, the book had to combine the insights of a wide range of practitioners. I am grateful, therefore, to mediators across the United States who critiqued this material. One of the most enjoyable aspects of this project was reviewing the pencil scratched manuscripts they returned to me. Although I take responsibility for *The Field Guide's* limitations, the suggestions and insights offered by the following people made this a better resource:

Maria Paz Avery: Education Development Center, Massachusetts
Patricia Barnes: Westchester Mediation Center, New York
Randy Compton: Colorado School Mediation Project, Colorado
John Conbere: John Conbere & Associates, Inc., Minnesota
Janice S. Countess: Peer Mediation Programs, Inc., New Jersey
Barbara Ann Davis: University of North Carolina at Asheville
Ellen "Bear" Hollyday: Constructive Conflict, Vermont
Ulric Johnson: Teens Against Gang Violence, Massachusetts
Daniel P. Joyce: Cleveland Mediation Center, Ohio
Nancy Kaplan: Conflict Resolution Unlimited, Washington
Sara Keeney: New Mexico Center for Dispute Resolution, New
    Mexico
Linda Lantieri: Resolving Conflict Creatively Program, New York
Paul Leite: Durfee High School, Massachusetts
Janet Patti: Hunter College, New York
Edna Povich: Center for Dispute Settlement, District of Columbia
Faye W. Wampler: FSR Associates, Virginia

Thank you to all the trainers who work with School Mediation Associates, and to Anna Kleinschmit-Kubasek for lighting up the office once a week.

Special thanks to Marla Zarrow for keeping SMA running smoothly, for insightful editing, and for sage advice always. And a warm welcome to Valerie Turner.

Thanks to my old friend Michael Weber of LeeWeber Design for designing the interior of this book, and to Alan Hill for his patience and wonderful cover design.

Thank you to many others who made contributions to *The School Mediator's Field Guide*, including but not limited to: Randy Compton for suggesting that I include the section on restorative justice in Chapter 2; Paul Hostovsky for information on interpreting; Marilyn Berman for the harassment letter idea; Howard Gadlin for his helpful article *"Careful Maneuvers: Mediating Sexual Harassment"* (Negotiation Journal, 7 (1991): 139-153); and my students at the University of Massachusetts.

Thank you to the co-mediators from whom I have learned so much over the years, especially Greg Williams, Cathy Eden, Francine Rondina, Nancy Grant and Joan Sokoloff. Thanks also to the many parties who accepted my help, told me their stories, and taught me so much.

Deepest thanks to my friends and family, especially Matt for last minute computer time, Trudy for taking care of Sam, Marty, Terry, Carol, Sam and Rachel (who is also a great editor).

As I finish this book, I realize how little of the material covered here I personally created. Thank you finally to the many individuals, known and unknown, who came before and who developed the strategies and theories upon which this work is based.

How To Use This Book

Please read through the introduction before you use *The School Mediator's Field Guide.*

Most chapters in this book include two types of information. First, chapters provide general information about the issues involved in each type of dispute. The more informed you are about the dynamics of sexual harassment, or large group conflicts, or prejudice, the more sensitive you will be in working with these conflicts. Secondly, each chapter offers concrete advice, based upon the actual experience of mediators, for modifying both the intake and the mediation process. These strategic adjustments will make you most effective for a particular case and enable you to best serve parties.

The Field Guide is designed to be used "in the field": the high pressure and often hectic offices and classrooms of the modern school. When confronted with a particular challenge, just turn to the corresponding chapter for assistance.

Many of the kinds of cases described in this volume are related, however. Cases involving homophobia often involve harassment, gangs conflicts often involve large groups, and so on. Relevant "companion" chapters are cited at the start of a number of chapters. You may initially want to read through the entire book to gain an overview of the cases and how they fit together.

It would be time consuming for someone preparing to mediate a conflict that involves sexual orientation harassment to also review related chapters on harassment, prejudice, and sexual harassment. A comprehensive checklist is therefore provided at the end of each chapter. The checklists outline key points to consider for each type of dispute, including relevant suggestions from other chapters in the book. Page numbers refer to more information about an item in a checklist (and serve as a kind of index). Review the checklist before you mediate a case.

Contents

Introduction

From being a mediator I learned that if people are willing to
talk and work things out, there is an answer to every problem.
If we were willing to talk more, the world would be a lot better.
                                        —*Middle school mediator*

[After you have been in mediation] you realize most people
should know this way of communicating. You realize the other
person thinks differently and there is usually a reason why they
acted in a certain way. Some of the people I thought I would
never like or even understand, I do. Even now we are friends.
It changed my whole outlook on them.
                                        —*High school disputant*

I use my mediation skills and outlook with my students, with my
colleagues, even at home. Mediation has made me a more
effective educator, and it has made our school a better place to
work and learn.
                                        —*High school teacher*

The practice of mediating interpersonal conflict is now common in North
American schools. Every school day, thousands of students and teachers
experience first-hand that with a little help, people in conflict can resolve
their differences peacefully. Typically, students and educators become mediators by participating in a mediation training offered at their school.
Following the basic mediation process introduced in their training, most are
able to help disputing peers resolve conflicts with considerable success.

School mediators regularly confront conflicts for which their basic training
does not adequately prepare them, however. Perhaps parties disagree about
a very sensitive issue, or there are large groups of parties rather than just
two, or the parties do not speak the same language. Significantly, these
cases represent daily challenges, not exceptions, for mediators.

The School Mediator's Field Guide is designed to help educators and students mediate these common yet challenging cases most effectively. Its purpose is to help school mediators:

- Understand the unique dynamics of a variety of difficult cases
- Determine whether a specific conflict is appropriate for mediation
- Assist parties in deciding whether to participate in mediation
- Strategically modify the mediation process to make it most effective for each case

The Field Guide is written for everyone who mediates in schools—counselors, teachers, students, administrators, community volunteers and others. The book will also be valuable to educators who "coordinate" school-based peer mediation programs. Readers who have completed at least a basic course in mediation and have experience mediating disputes in schools will gain the most from this book.

For purposes of *The Field Guide*, mediation is defined as:[*]

> *a structured method of conflict resolution in which individuals assist people in dispute by listening to their concerns and helping them negotiate. Six fundamental pillars of mediation are:*

1. **Voluntariness**
   Parties choose to participate in mediation. Once the process begins, they choose whether and how to resolve their dispute. Parties are free to conclude the mediation process at any time and pursue other means of resolving their conflict.

2. **Impartiality**
   Mediators refrain from demonstrating judgment about right and wrong and strive to be unbiased in their practice at all times. They

---

[*] As the mediation field has grown from its diffuse roots, mediators have developed different approaches to their work. Though every mediator may not agree with this definition—especially the inclusion of interpersonal transformation as a fundamental pillar—*The Field Guide* is informed by this approach to mediation.

also have no power or interest in forcing parties to take any particular action. When agreements are created, they are fashioned according to the needs of the parties.*

3. **Confidentiality**

   Information that is shared during mediation is held in the strictest confidence by mediators and coordinators. Parties are informed of any exceptions to confidentiality—typically information that is dangerous or illegal—before they begin the process.

4. **Interpersonal Transformation**

   A primary goal of mediation is to create a forum where people in conflict can come to a greater appreciation of their own strengths as well as acknowledge other parties' concerns.[1] Mediators help parties create agreements that resolve specific issues in dispute, but whenever possible, these agreements grow out of parties' increased understanding of themselves and willingness to understand others.

5. **Self-Determination**

   During mediation, parties are encouraged to take responsibility for their actions in the past and for their behavior in the future. Mediators help parties manage the process as well, intervening only when necessary and relinquishing control as soon as parties can effectively negotiate on their own. Regardless of their role in the conflict, all parties participate in creating a resolution to the dispute.

6. **Safety**

   Mediators create an environment that is physically and emotionally safe. In this way parties can honestly express their thoughts and feelings and develop trust in the mediators and the process. Mediation can work to its potential only in an environment that maintains the dignity of all participants.

When any of the six fundamental principles of mediation are compromised,

> THE MEETING OF TWO PERSONALITIES IS LIKE THE CONTACT OF TWO CHEMICAL SUBSTANCES. IF THERE IS ANY REACTION, BOTH ARE TRANSFORMED.
>
> CARL JUNG

---

* Increasingly, mediators use the words "impartial" or "unbiased" instead of "neutral" because the former words connote an active task and the last a passive state of being. No mediator is completely neutral: all have conscious opinions and beliefs as well as unconscious assumptions that influence their practice. The mediator's job is to energetically and attentively work to uncover his or her assumptions and remain unbiased.

mediators should either terminate their efforts or at least not label the intervention "mediation."

It is important to understand that the school environment presents obstacles to upholding these principles. The primary challenge concerns school discipline. Using institutional power to force students to comply with school norms, the disciplinary system plays an important role in school life. Many times mediation and discipline work in parallel on the same conflict: parties receive disciplinary consequences *and* participate in mediation. But these efforts must remain separate or the effectiveness of each will be diminished. Disciplinarians must ensure that school rules are non-negotiable even though parties may participate in mediation. School mediators must preserve the integrity of their empowering services while working alongside the usually coercive disciplinary system.

School administrators especially need to appreciate the strengths and limitations of mediation and how their position restricts their ability to truly mediate school conflicts. Parties—staff as well as students—may not feel safe discussing their difficulties with someone who can (and often will) punish them. And because disciplinarians must uphold school rules, it is difficult for them to be unbiased. Exceptional disciplinarians overcome these obstacles, but it usually makes sense for administrators to refer appropriate conflicts to be mediated by others.[*]

* * *

This book is focused exclusively on mediating interpersonal and intergroup conflicts that occur *in schools*, where the physical setting and the parties are relatively constant. As a result, the similarities in how different mediators approach each of these challenging conflicts are as instructive as the differences. Though there are many variations, most school mediators utilize a

---

[*] Because most school-based mediation is done by counselors, teachers or students, this book is written from the perspective of educators who are not administrators.

series of structured and relatively basic steps like the ones below:

A. **Intake Interview**: A mediation "coordinator" (usually an adult) meets with parties, answers their questions about mediation, and helps them decide whether they would like to try the process. If they do, the coordinator selects appropriate mediators and schedules a session to occur as soon as possible.*

B. **Mediation Session**: An individual mediator or more often a pair of "co-mediators" meet with parties together in a so-called "joint session." This begins the formal mediation process. Most mediation sessions include some version of the following steps:

 1. **Welcome the Parties**: Mediators describe the process, set ground rules, answer questions, and confirm parties' willingness to participate.

 2. **Discover the Stories**: Each party is given an opportunity to describe the situation without interruption. Mediators listen with concern and summarize each party's presentation.

 3. **Dig Deeper**: Mediators ask questions of parties to uncover feelings and clarify differing perceptions. Parties are encouraged to communicate directly and ask each other questions as well. The goal is to help parties understand one another and their situation as completely as possible.

 4. **Optional Private Sessions and Caucuses**: Sometimes mediators meet with each party separately while the other party (or parties) waits outside. There are many reasons to hold such "privates sessions." They enable mediators to explore sensitive issues in depth, and they enable parties to modify positions and share private information while "saving face." Between private sessions, co-mediators confer or "caucus" with each other without either party present.

---

* In this book, the individual who does the logistical work involved in arranging for and following up on mediation sessions is referred to as the "coordinator." In most school mediation programs, the coordinator and the person who eventually mediates a dispute are different people. School-based mediators who are not part of a formal mediation program do this coordination work themselves, functioning effectively as both coordinator and mediator.

5. **Building Understanding and Agreement**: Here mediators turn parties toward the future and ask *what they want* in order to resolve the conflict. The parties brainstorm possible solutions and with the mediators' assistance, negotiate a settlement to their dispute.

6. **Agreement Writing and Closing**: If parties have been able to resolve their conflict, the mediators highlight areas of understanding, write down the terms of agreement, and have parties sign the agreement. Agreement or not, mediators end the session by thanking parties and offering their services in the future. Sometimes parties are referred to other school programs; most often they return to class or their job.

C. **Follow-Up Interview**: Coordinators and/or mediators contact parties to make sure their agreement is working and to offer assistance. Follow-up interviews take place anywhere from one day to two weeks after the mediation session, depending upon the nature of the dispute and what occurred during the mediation session.

* * *

Many readers will benefit from reviewing my first book, *Students Resolving Conflict: Peer Mediation in Schools* (GoodYear/Addison Wesley, 1995). Although *The Field Guide* stands alone, it is also a companion to that earlier book, in that many subjects mentioned in passing in this volume are explained in detail there. That book also addresses the considerable *programmatic* challenges of implementing and maintaining school-based mediation programs.

Readers who do not have a peer mediation program in their schools may want to consider implementing one. In this popular program, a diverse group of students and staff are trained to mediate disputes that occur among their peers. Ideally this includes mediating conflicts not only among stu-

dents, but between teachers and students and among teachers.* The reported benefits of peer mediation programs include an 85% rate of effectiveness,
a reduction in suspensions, building the life skills and self-esteem of mediators, and an improvement in school climate.

A healthy peer mediation program will also benefit any individual's effort to
mediate the difficult conflicts discussed in this book. In schools that have a
peer mediation program:

- All members of the school community (students, teachers, administrators, parents, support staff) will likely be familiar with mediation.
- Administrators and teachers should understand what is required to
  make mediation work in the school setting.
- Student and staff mediators are continually honing their mediation skills and might be capable of mediating especially
  challenging conflicts.
- Potential parties may have already participated in a mediation session and therefore have faith in the process.

* * *

Mediation services—whether provided by students or staff—are a wonderful
addition to any school. The process prevents conflicts from escalating, urges
parties towards a greater understanding of themselves and others, and assists
parties in creating workable solutions to their disputes. But mediation is
not a panacea for the problem of conflict in schools. Societal stresses such
as poverty, prejudice and family disintegration, to name just a few, exacer-
bate this problem and are largely beyond educators' control.

The good news, however, is that as institutions whose mission is to *educate*,
schools are uniquely suited to minimize the incidence of the conflicts discussed in this book. A range of increasingly common educational

> FORTUNATELY, ANALY-
> SIS IS NOT THE ONLY
> WAY TO RESOLVE
> INNER CONFLICTS.
> LIFE ITSELF STILL
> REMAINS A VERY
> EFFECTIVE THERAPIST.
> KAREN HORNEY

---

* A school's willingness to encourage teachers as well as students to use mediation indicates
  an embrace of the process that bodes well for any school-based mediation effort.

practices—teaching conflict resolution skills to all students and staff, reducing student-teacher ratios, utilizing cooperative learning strategies, implementing community service learning, establishing democratic school governance—can work *within* schools to create a more productive and "peaceable" environment. In addition, mediators who identify "conflict patterns" that indicate systemic problems can take the lead and design curricular units for students, conduct professional development presentations for staff, or facilitate community forums addressing topics (prejudice, conflict resolution skills, sexual harassment, etc.) that are of concern. Mediation services should ideally be *one part of a comprehensive effort* to minimize the incidence of conflict, encourage academic success, and make schools safe.

* * *

One final, extremely important, and multi-faceted point: *Be cautious* when mediating the conflicts described in this book:

1. **Make sure you have the support of school administrators.** When administrators understand the process, they can make logistical obstacles disappear; when they don't, they may destroy mediation by coercing parties to try it or punishing parties more harshly if they fail to resolve their conflict. Administrative support is crucial when mediating cases that involve sensitive, potentially explosive issues like the ones described here.
2. **Choose mediators carefully.** Young people have effectively served as mediators for more benign examples of every kind of conflict described in this book. But as disputes become more challenging, and for the more difficult categories of cases like those involving large groups, sexual harassment, or parents and children, use adult-student teams or adults only as mediators.*

A MIND THAT IS STRETCHED BY A NEW EXPERIENCE CAN NEVER GO BACK TO ITS OLD DIMENSIONS

OLIVER WENDELL HOLMES

---

* I do not want to appear biased against young people. There is no simple correlation between age and mediation ability; skilled student mediators are more effective than most untrained adults and many trained adults. When all else is equal, however, the experience, sensitivity and confidence that skilled adult mediators possess make them preferable to student mediators for the most difficult cases.

3. **Assess your own skills.** Misconceptions abound about what mediators do, and many teachers and administrators who arbitrate student conflicts confuse that practice with mediating. If you have not participated in a legitimate mediation training, please consider doing so before intervening in the complex cases described in this book. School mediation trainings run between 15 and 30 hours and emphasize roleplays in which participants mediate mock disputes and receive feedback from experienced practitioners. School Mediation Associates (SMA), which I direct, is the oldest organization devoted to school-based mediation and one of many organizations across North America that conduct such trainings. Contact SMA at:

> School Mediation Associates
> 134-B Standish Road, Watertown, MA 02472
> (617) 926-5969/web site: www.schoolmediation.com

The Conflict Resolution Education Network (CREnet), an excellent clearinghouse and membership organization, can provide information about resources in your area. CREnet can be reached at:

> The Conflict Resolution Education Network
> 1527 New Hampshire Avenue NW, Washington, DC 20036
> (202) 667-9700/web site: www.crenet.org

4. **Get help when you need it.** If there is a school mediation organization or a community mediation program in your area, chances are that they would be happy to consult about a particularly challenging case. In addition, these programs might be willing to assist with programmatic issues such as raising funds and administering peer mediation programs.[*]

5. **Remember: It is OK to say no.** If you don't feel qualified to handle a particular case, if you don't have access to the right mediators, or if the details of a conflict convince you that mediation would be inappropriate,

---

[*] Using local mediators can also overcome one of the limitations of this book: that the information provided here, though influenced by mediators across North America, was ultimately filtered through one mediator's lens of time, place and personality.

...TO KNOW THAT
EVEN ONE LIFE HAS
BREATHED EASIER
BECAUSE YOU HAVE
LIVED—THIS IS TO
HAVE SUCCEEDED.
RALPH WALDO EMERSON

it is your responsibility to *decline to intervene*. Help the parties find other forms of assistance, but don't put yourself, your mediators, the parties, or your mediation program at risk.

* * *

School-based mediators face challenges every day. People are unpredictable, and ultimately one never knows what is going to happen in a mediation session. Though it is impossible to eliminate all of the risks associated with this rewarding work, *The School Mediator's Field Guide* should help you understand the risks and take steps to minimize them. Mediation is a powerful process that enables people to dramatically change their lives for the better. I hope this book enables you to provide that opportunity to those involved in even the most difficult conflicts.

March 1999   Richard Cohen
                                                   Watertown, Massachusetts

I would be delighted to hear from you if you know of strategies or other information that would make *The School Mediator's Field Guide* a better resource. Contact me at School Mediation Associates.

1

MEDIATING
CONFLICTS
INVOLVING
PREJUDICE

Jesse was playing games at computer terminal three in his school's computer room. He was in a bad mood because he had flunked his math test. Quang, a Vietnamese boy, had reserved time on the same computer. Jesse never liked Quang; in fact, he felt uncomfortable with all the Asian students in his school. He thought they acted like girls. When Quang asked Jesse to get up, explaining that it was his time to use the computer, Jesse just sat there and ignored him. Eventually Quang began to move Jesse's books. Jesse jumped up and shouted: "Don't touch my stuff, chink!" The computer teacher separated them immediately.

Conflicts involving prejudice are a common occurrence in many schools. So-called "racial" conflicts are not a new problem for North American educators, but many feel they are occurring with more frequency. Of the complex factors that have led to this increase, the most fundamental is that the United States and Canada now have the most heterogeneous student body ever. Some urban schools have as many as eighty different ethnic backgrounds represented among their students, and even rural school districts report more diversity than in the past.

Cultural diversity represents a resource of tremendous potential for educators. What better way to learn about different cultures than from your peers and their families? What better way to become a conscientious citizen of a shrinking world than to learn and work with peers who reflect the world's diversity? But differences, when misunderstood or disrespected, can lead to problems, not the least of which are interpersonal conflicts. People have prejudices, and when they act upon them, insensitive behavior, discrimination or explicit harassment can result. Mediation can effectively help students and adults resolve these conflicts involving prejudice.

What are Conflicts Involving Prejudice?

Prejudice literally means to "pre-judge." Some degree of prejudice is involved in almost every interpersonal conflict, regardless of the issues in dispute. For our purposes, prejudice can be defined as:

> *An adverse judgment towards members of a particular group formed without knowledge or examination of the facts.*[2]

Two elements of this definition are especially important to the relationship of conflicts involving prejudice and mediation. The first is that prejudice *is not based upon fact*. It is created from misinformation, misinterpretation, and stereotype—not from personal knowledge or experience. Prejudice is therefore logically as well as morally wrong.

WE HATE SOME PERSONS BECAUSE WE DO NOT KNOW THEM; AND WILL NOT KNOW THEM BECAUSE WE HATE THEM.

CHARLES CALEB COLTON

The second element is that prejudice *requires a depersonalized "other" as its target*. The prejudiced person assumes that simply because an individual is African-American, female, or Muslim, that individual must be lazy, weak, or a terrorist, respectively. He can project these false assumptions only upon those whom he does not know well. Prejudice flourishes only when these two elements —misinformation and depersonalization—are present.

"Conflicts involving prejudice" are disputes in which one individual acts with hostility towards another individual in part because of the latter's membership in a particular group. The most familiar groups are defined by race, ethnic background, gender, religion, class and sexual orientation. In addition, young people delineate many other age-related and school specific groups including the grade, clique, former school, athletic team, neighborhood, gang, club, section of the cafeteria, and manner of dress with which another student is affiliated. Membership in a group can be the result of personal choice (how one dresses or who one chooses as friends), a matter of chance (which neighborhood one grew up in or what grade one attends) or determined by birth (being Chinese, black, female, Jewish, etc.).

Students act upon their prejudices in a range of ways. Sometimes merely voicing them leads to interpersonal conflicts. But more often prejudices are expressed through teasing, dirty looks, gossiping, name-calling, physical aggression, harassment and other hostile behavior. Often conflicts involving prejudice include actions that would be considered illegal in the US under the Civil Rights Act of 1964.

Is Prejudice Involved?

The overwhelming majority of interpersonal conflicts in schools occur between students of the same race and background. Of the school-based conflicts that do involve prejudice, only a small percentage involve prejudice as the primary issue. (An example of such a conflict is when two girls harass another student whom they don't know simply because she is a "preppie.") More often prejudice is a contributing issue or undercurrent, not the main source of conflict. Prejudice might force a conflict towards its climax, or it might surface only after the conflict has erupted over other issues. As a result, it can be difficult to tell what part prejudice has played in a dispute. Let's look at two examples.

> *Tony and Shawn, Caucasian boys, are not friends. Although they are in some classes together, they hardly know each other. Recently Tony has seen Shawn giving him dirty looks. When Tony mentioned this to his friends, they convinced him that Shawn wanted to fight him. Their simmering conflict reached the boiling point when Shawn intentionally stepped on some*

papers that Tony dropped in class. The two boys immediately threatened one another. The teacher acted quickly and was able to calm them for the remainder of the class. The mediation coordinator learned of this dispute from a "request for mediation" slip that Tony dropped in a mediation referral box.

* * *

Eleana and Shanika, a Latina and an African-American girl, respectively, have attended school together since grammar school. At times they would have called each other friends. Recently the two had a disagreement over their roles in the school play. They began trading put-downs and threats, some of which had a racial tone. The threats became increasingly serious until a fight was planned, with many of the girls' friends lining up to participate. Most of Eleana's friends are Hispanic. Most of Shanika's are black. The assistant principal learned of the conflict from the drama coach, who said that a large group of black girls were planning to fight an equally large group of Hispanic girls after school.

At first glance, it appears that the second conflict is motivated by prejudice while the first one is not. Appearances can be deceiving, however. Shawn and Tony live in contiguous neighborhoods in their town. Shawn's neighborhood, called "the Tracks," is working class and predominantly Irish. Tony lives in a more fashionable, upper middle class neighborhood called "Village Heights." A great rivalry has existed for many years between their two neighborhoods, pre-dating their births. Neither had been actively involved in this class tension in the past, but both, especially Shawn, were motivated in part by prejudicial feelings. Shawn's friends had urged him to "beat on a 'Heights.'" Just below the surface, prejudice played a crucial role in motivating this conflict.

In Eleana and Shanika's dispute, on the other hand, prejudice was hardly a factor at all. Their conflict had more to do with a clash of personalities and old wounds from elementary school. (Shanika felt that Eleana was "showing off" in the play and getting all of the attention.) As is not unusual, many of the girls' friends were of the same race as themselves, and so it appeared that "racial" groups were lining up against each other. But this particular conflict was not motivated by prejudice. Both girls appeared very comfortable with the other's race. Eleana's boyfriend was even African-American.

Prejudices can be express topics of disagreement, or they can be concealed behind other issues. They may be discussed by parties in a joint session, or they may be alluded to only in private. Even when it seems clear that prejudice is a factor, the parties may not admit to this: Mediators regularly conclude sessions not knowing whether and to what degree a conflict was fueled by prejudice. Mediators must therefore remain alert in this regard. Be prepared to discover prejudice where you least expect it and not find it where you had assumed it would be.

How Mediation Can Help

Mediation has the potential to facilitate communication and heal relationships across even the largest chasms of misunderstanding and hostility. An implicit goal of every mediation session, regardless of the part prejudice plays in the dispute, is to help parties understand one another. Parties discuss issues like teasing, stolen property, or rumors, and simultaneously, and often despite themselves, they begin to listen to and tacitly respect one another.

For conflicts involving prejudice, the implicit goal of mutual understanding becomes primary. Mediation helps parties focus on how they feel and what they experienced; the facilitation of dialogue takes precedence over the formulation of concrete agreements. Statements such as: "I felt hurt and angry when you said that because I have had to deal with that kind of attitude my whole life" are the currency of the exchange. At a minimum, parties hear what the other has to say. Although occasionally one party may accuse another of "playing the race card," often parties come to understand and possibly even empathize with the experience of their supposed adversary.

One of the things that victims of prejudice and harassment want most, in addition to the behavior never happening again, is for the "perpetrator" to understand the impact of their behavior and apologize for their actions. When injured parties receive an acknowledgment of their suffering, they can begin to "close" the experience and move on with their lives. Mediation encourages this type of exchange.

WE WANT PEOPLE TO
FEEL WITH US MORE
THAN TO ACT FOR US.
GEORGE ELIOT

It is also important to stress that, when it comes to prejudice, mediation can work *in spite of* the parties. This is one of the curious paradoxes in a process that strives to empower parties whenever possible. For even if the prejudiced party does not empathize with the aggrieved party, mediation weakens the two foundations of prejudice discussed above: misinformation and depersonalization. Parties in a mediation session participate in a shared, intimate experience. They have immediate and constructive contact with one another, contact that by its very nature can contradict stereotypes and replace misinformation with first-hand knowledge. Participation in the process, therefore, in itself represents a kind of victory. And this holds true even if the issues of prejudice are not openly identified or conceded. Let's look at another example:

> Bob, a self-described "skinhead" and the leader of a small clique of his peers, was harassing another student named Paul. Paul was one of the only Jewish students in the rural high school they both attended. Bob would call Paul anti-Semitic names whenever he passed. The harassment became more disturbing when Bob and his friends began drawing swastikas and taping pictures of concentration camp victims on Paul's locker. Paul finally went to speak with the school disciplinarian about the situation. The disciplinarian spoke with each boy separately, and he punished Bob severely for his offensive behavior. He also referred them both to the school's peer mediation program.

> During the mediation session that followed, Paul haltingly described his concerns while Bob looked away. The harassment

had been going on for years in a variety of forms. When it was Bob's turn to speak, he claimed that Paul often smiled when they were teasing him. He thought that Paul didn't mind the teasing. Much later, in a private session, Bob admitted that he had been teased when he was younger and that this had upset him very much. Although Bob never let his guard down completely, in the end he agreed to stop bothering Paul. Both boys agreed to go their separate ways.

Ten days later the mediators received a letter from Paul saying how pleased he was with mediation. Bob and Bob's friends were not teasing him anymore, and Paul said that mediation was "the best thing I have ever experienced" to resolve this on-going problem.

As always, there is no guarantee that mediation will be effective in resolving a particular conflict. And having students participate in mediation should not imply that they will not receive appropriate consequences when they violate school rules. In situations like the one above, where Bob's harassment was explicit and even vicious, mediation may be utilized *in addition* to punitive disciplinary action taken by the administration. But as Paul's letter indicated, mediation can play an important role in helping students understand themselves and others, modify their behavior, and resolve conflicts involving prejudice. Mediation impresses upon parties the human consequences of their actions in a way that only the most psychologically defended can resist. People rarely walk away unchanged.

The Challenge of Mediating Conflicts Involving Prejudice

Conflicts involving prejudice present some unique difficulties to school mediators. In addition to sharing many of the characteristics of conflicts that involve harassment outlined in the next chapter, a few elements typical of these conflicts include:

- **Non-Negotiable Values and Beliefs.** Conflicts that are driven by differing values and beliefs can be the most difficult to resolve. Beliefs are deeply held and non-negotiable; they cannot be traded or exchanged. It

Prejudice

is ludicrous to think of a person saying: "I will stop believing that your race is inferior if you return my money." Beliefs *can* be modified and transformed, however, and prejudicial beliefs, based as they are upon false information, are especially susceptible to modification. This is where the hope and the strength of the mediation process lies. But it is much more common for parties to change their behavior rather than their attitudes and beliefs after participating in mediation.

- **A Profound Emotional Component.** Issues of prejudice engender strong feelings in parties, and mediators must be comfortable with powerful displays of emotion. Mediators need to be confident facilitators of the process because unintentional outbursts and disruptions are likely.

Suggestions for Mediating Conflicts Involving Prejudice

Mediators need to make small yet important modifications to their work when mediating conflicts involving prejudice. The coordination of these cases, the expectations of the mediators and the parties, and the mediation process itself can all be affected. Consider the following suggestions:

Intake

- **First and foremost, get parties to the session.** Often a mediator or coordinator suspects that prejudice is influencing a dispute, but the parties do not mention the issue during the intake interview. Aside from asking non-threatening questions in order to bring the prejudice to the surface ("Are there any other reasons why he might be bothering you?" or "Do you know if he teases other Asian students?"), it is best to take one's cues from the parties. Schedule the session to address the issues that they present; pushing parties to acknowledge prejudice before they are ready will scare them away. Disputants will raise these issues in the safety of the mediation session if they are important. Comments like: "All of her people are like that" or "He is always picking on kids in my neighborhood" can be used by the mediators to initiate a conversation about prejudice. Remember too that participation in the mediation process can help to reduce prejudices even if they are never explicitly discussed. The first goal should be to get parties into the session.

- **Avoid labeling disputes.** A common error is to label conflicts with the phrase "racial dispute." As noted, a conflict between students of two different races is not necessarily a "racial dispute." Both parties and mediators suffer when this and similar labels are used. Parties are demeaned because the motivations that resulted in their conflict are reduced to an odious, and sometimes erroneous, label. This label can follow them into the mediation session and beyond. Mediators suffer because they can lose their composure when mediating a "racial" dispute and end up looking for issues that aren't there and missing those that are.

As always, mediators should learn from the parties themselves what has motivated their conflict. Yet there is nothing wrong with alerting mediators that prejudice might be an issue in a particular dispute. If more needs to be said, coordinators can inform mediators of the specific information that indicates that prejudice may be a factor. Labels are entirely counter-productive, however. Educate referral sources like administrators and teachers about labeling as well.

> LIGHT CAME TO ME WHEN I REALIZED THAT I DID NOT HAVE TO CONSIDER ANY RACIAL GROUP AS A WHOLE. GOD MADE THEM DUCK BY DUCK AND THAT WAS THE ONLY WAY I COULD SEE THEM.
>
> ZORA NEALE HURSTON

Mediator Selection

- **Train mediators to be comfortable handling conflicts involving prejudice.** All mediators can benefit from training designed to prepare them to handle conflicts involving prejudice. Training can be provided either as a part of the initial training or in the form of advanced training. Information covered can include:
  —General information about prejudice: what it is; how prejudices are created and transmitted; how, with the addition of social power, prejudice becomes discrimination and oppression; and so on.
  —A personal exploration of mediators' own stereotypes and prejudices.
  —The dynamics of prejudice in mediation, including the fact that prejudice is often present in interpersonal conflict, methods to

uncover it when it is, and methods to work with prejudice once it is openly expressed.

—The reminder that although mediators use a more subtle, indirect method to eliminate prejudice while they mediate, they can speak out against prejudice and work to end discrimination of all kinds when not mediating.

- **Choose mediators wisely.** The challenging nature of conflicts involving prejudice requires mediators who are confident and mature, who have examined their own biases, and who can handle strong emotions. Usually the most capable student mediators are used. Adult-student teams or even adult teams of mediators should work with the most difficult cases, especially in middle schools. Beware of becoming dependent upon the adults, however. Students may not mediate with the sophistication of a more experienced adult, but much of the time they get the job done as effectively.

  Matching key characteristics of the mediators with those of the parties, or "mirroring," is essential when assigning mediators to a conflict involving prejudice. If the dispute involves gender bias, try to schedule a male/female team to mediate. If the conflict involves a Haitian and an African-American, ideally a Haitian and an African-American mediator would be assigned to the case. Although there is some debate regarding just how essential mirroring is, there is no question that it can be an important factor in building the parties' trust in the mediators, and consequently in the process. Mediators who mirror key characteristics of the parties also provide a compelling demonstration of how members of these groups can work collaboratively. If the school has a peer mediation program, the diversity of the student trainees will be a boon in this regard.

During the Session

- For conflicts involving prejudice, the primary goal of mediation is to increase communication and mutual understanding. Written agreements are secondary.

• Conflicts involving prejudice seriously test a mediator's ability to be unbiased and listen accurately. Guard against responding inappropriately by "preaching" to parties. Instead, help them come to terms with the existence and the impact of prejudice.

Final Cautions

Although it is challenge enough to actually mediate conflicts involving prejudice, school-based mediators must also be wary of misapplying the process in their schools. Serious problems have been identified regarding the way that mediation has been integrated into a school's systemic response to prejudice, problems which are wholly separate from the mediation process itself. Two of the most common difficulties in this regard are discussed below. These difficulties are related, and working to solve one will necessarily make an improvement in the other.

NEVER TRY TO REASON THE PREJUDICE OUT OF A MAN. IT WAS NOT REASONED INTO HIM, AND CANNOT BE REASONED OUT.

SYDNEY SMITH

The school mediation effort is integrated into an already discriminatory conflict management system.

Every school has its own culture and unique approach to education. When mediators work in a school, their efforts are significantly affected by this culture. It is the foundation upon which they work.

A school's culture is often taken for granted by those who have worked within an institution for many years. To an outsider, however, it is quite striking. An experienced educator can tour a school for one day and get a credible impression of the way that school functions. Does it promote rigid authority from the top or personal responsibility at all levels? Does it focus solely on academics or integrate other experiences into the educational process? What seems to be the quality and the tenor of relationships between staff and students? Among staff members? Does the school have a bright, creative atmosphere or does it feel drab and stultifying?

The culture of a school also prescribes its relationship to prejudice. Unfortunately, in many North American schools there exists a destructive element of prejudice. This should not be surprising: Public schools mirror the society in which they function. All of the "isms" that afflict a society—racism, sexism, anti-Semitism, heterosexism, ageism—make their presence felt in a society's schools as well.

North American educators, with very few exceptions, do not strive to teach their students to be prejudiced. If anything, education professionals lead the struggle to eradicate discrimination of all kinds. But many well-meaning teachers and administrators have prejudices themselves, and when they do their jobs, they exercise these prejudices. Given the considerable degree of social control that educators have over the lives of students, this can result in practices that discriminate against specific individuals or groups.

Mediators and coordinators must be vigilant about ensuring that their efforts do not buttress discriminatory patterns that exist in a school. Two examples follow that illustrate how mediators found themselves doing just that.

Example A
Some suburban towns offer students from a nearby city the opportunity to attend their schools. The rationale is that the urban students will receive a higher quality education in the suburban schools than in the embattled, under-funded schools in their own communities. Often the population of these suburban communities is predominantly white, while the young people bussed out from the inner city are students of color (mostly black and Hispanic).

Upon implementing peer mediation programs in a number of these suburban schools, program coordinators noticed that the city students, and specifically black students, were encouraged to mediate more often than white students. In addition, disputes involving African-Americans were routinely deemed "serious," with administrators and teachers requesting that adult instead of student mediators be used. After mediating these cases, however, adult mediators would report that the disputes were no more "serious" in nature than typical student disputes.

Something was wrong. It turned out that the suburban teachers were less comfortable, some were even fearful, of the black students. Their own prejudices and lack of experience with urban youth led them to misinterpret black students' behavior. Identical actions taken by black and white students were deemed more serious when taken by the former. This culture of prejudice led to discrimination against the African-American students in many aspects of school life. Until this pattern was discovered, the mediation program was an unwitting accomplice to the system's discrimination.

Example B

For a peer mediation program to be effective, it is essential to have peer mediators who represent the diversity of the student body. All races, cliques, age groups, etc. should be included. Experienced mediation trainers explain this in detail to schools before they begin to implement a mediation program. More than once, however, mediators have arrived at a school to conduct a training only to find that in spite of their advice, the school has selected a homogeneous group of students to be trained. Trainees have all been of the same race and background, and sometimes even all belong to the same clique (academically oriented, well-adjusted, student government) in the school. Not only do these mediation programs begin at a disadvantage, they implicitly support a discriminatory system.

These examples illustrate how prejudice can be evidenced systematically in a school. Such institutional biases compromise the effectiveness and the reputation of a mediation effort. Mediation coordinators in these schools had to approach their administrators, describe their concerns, and help to facilitate change. The warning illustrated by the examples is clear. When it comes to prejudice, mediators must guard against becoming part of the problem rather than part of the solution.

The mediation effort is used as the solitary tool to decrease prejudice and promote harmony at school.

> *Carol and Maura were two friends who had the same English class. A few months ago, Carol found out that Maura was gay.*

[RACISM] IS A SHADOW OVER ALL OF US, AND THE SHADOW IS DARKEST OVER THOSE WHO FEEL IT LEAST AND ALLOW ITS EVIL EFFECTS TO GO ON.

PEARL BUCK

*From then on the two girls frequently hurled "friendly" slurs
about the other's sexual orientation back and forth. The insulting went on for many weeks in front of teachers and fellow students. Eventually, Maura lost her temper and the friends got
into a physical confrontation. A mediation session followed in
which they came to understand how their "playing" had gotten
out of hand and begun to hurt each other, especially Maura.
Among their questions as the session came to its conclusion was:
Why had the teacher let them insult each other openly for so long?*

This story illustrates a final caution. Carol and Maura were teasing each
other with barbs created from misinformation and prejudice. This should
be cause for concern in any school. Yet their teachers regarded the students'
behavior neither as an opportunity to teach about prejudice nor as a violation of school or classroom norms. The students received no feedback from
the institution until they violated a different school rule: the prohibition
against physical fighting.

Prejudice can operate on many levels within a school and affect everything
from student performance and curriculum to class assignment and discipline. Efforts to eliminate prejudice consequently have to be multi-leveled,
long-term, and ongoing. Some schools, often in reaction to a dramatic sur-
facing of racial or ethnic tension, rush to find something they can do immediately. Because school-based mediation is an effective and visible tool,
implementing a mediation program is often where they start. The problem
is, it is often where they stop. Starting a mediation effort is a commendable
step, but it is only one among an array of actions that must be taken if prejudice is to be reduced in a school. The following additional interventions
should be considered when creating a comprehensive program to reduce
prejudice and discrimination:

- **Human Relations/Appreciation of Diversity Task Force:**
  Although the last thing many schools want is another committee, a
  task force can effectively oversee the prejudice reduction effort. The
  group should be as diverse as possible to ensure that a variety of

perspectives are represented. It can include administrators, teachers, students, and parents. Its task: to critically examine the institution and create policies that work to eliminate all forms of racism, prejudice and discrimination.

- **School Mission:** It is of primary importance to create, disseminate, and support a school philosophy that values diversity, respects difference of opinion, promotes self esteem and cultural pride, and encourages safety and trust.

- **Staff Development:** Most teachers and administrators were educated in schools that were homogeneous by today's standards. Contemporary students who have grown up with "all kinds of people" are sometimes more comfortable with diversity than their teachers. Training for staff can include personal exploration of prejudice, information about specific groups in the school, an introduction to curricula and methods of teaching about difference, and practical skill development regarding how to defuse acts of prejudice and discrimination in school. The sensitive nature of this type of training makes it advisable to utilize experienced trainers.

- **Multi-Cultural Curriculum:** Multi-culturalism in schools is still a point of clamorous debate as of this writing. It seems certain, however, that schools will increasingly modify their curriculum to represent a more diverse perspective on history, literature, and all academic subjects. This trend can only contribute to a decrease of prejudice in schools.

- **Cooperative Learning:** Encourage teachers to use cooperative learning techniques in the classroom. Research has shown that simply requiring students to work collaboratively reduces prejudice. Be sure to train teachers to use cooperative learning effectively, however: If teachers do not adequately prepare students to work together, this practice just reinforces their stereotypes.

- **Employ a diverse staff at all levels of the school:** When school staff reflect the diversity of the student body—and when students witness the staff working well together—it provides a powerful message about the worth of *all* people in the building.

- **Hold special programs, assemblies, and educational events** for students that celebrate diversity, promote group pride, encourage personal interaction between members of different groups, contradict stereotypes, and strengthen students' ability to stand up for their beliefs. Such programs should be fresh, experientially based, and non-didactic.

Mediation is one of the most effective processes for resolving conflicts involving prejudice that occur in schools. Little else can equal its ability to increase understanding between parties in dispute. Mediation will not on its own end the complex problem of prejudice and discrimination in schools, and mediation efforts must guard against systemic abuses. But mediation can heal wounds that result from prejudice and make conflict a learning—even a transformative—experience.

Resources

Organizations

Anti-Defamation League of B'nai B'rith, National Office
823 UN Plaza
New York, NY 10017
(212) 490-2525
web site: www.adl.org

National Conference for Community and Justice
71 Fifth Avenue, Suite 1100
New York, NY 10003
(212) 206-0006

Facing History and Ourselves
16 Hurd Road
Brookline, MA 02146
(617) 232-1595
email: info-boston@facing.org

Southern Poverty Law Center
Teaching Tolerance - Klanwatch - Militia Task Force
400 Washington Avenue
Montgomery, AL 36104
(334) 264-0286

Community Relations Service (CRS)
Department of Justice
600 E. Street, NW, Suite 2000
Washington, DC 20530
(202) 305-2935
The US Federal government's "peacemaker" for community conflicts
and tensions rising from difference in race, color, and national origin,
provides experienced mediators to local communities

World of Difference/Anti-Defamation League
126 High Street
Boston, MA 02110
(617) 457-8800

Prejudice

Checklist
MEDIATING CONFLICTS INVOLVING PREJUDICE

INTAKE

✓ Don't push parties to acknowledge prejudice before they are ready: It will scare them away (30)

✓ Avoid labeling conflicts as "racial disputes" (31)

MEDIATOR SELECTION

✓ Choose mediators who (32):
- Are confident and mature
- Have examined their own biases
- Can handle strong emotions

✓ Use mediators who share key characteristics with, or "mirror," the parties (32)

✓ Use the most capable student mediators or adult-student teams (adult teams for the most difficult cases) (32)

DURING THE SESSION

✓ Strive to engender mutual understanding by helping parties focus on how they feel and what they experienced (27)

✓ Focus on facilitating dialogue more than formulating concrete agreements (27)

✓ When appropriate, ask non-threatening questions in order to bring potential prejudice to the surface (30)

✓ Be careful not to "preach" to parties; instead, help them come to terms with the existence and the impact of prejudice (33)

✓ Monitor your feelings for biases that might prevent you from being effective (31)

✓ Take private sessions when necessary (64)

CAUTION! ENSURE THAT:

✓ The mediation effort is not integrated into an already discriminatory conflict management system (33)

✓ The mediation effort is not the solitary tool to decrease prejudice and promote harmony at school (35)

MEDIATING CONFLICTS INVOLVING HARASSMENT: AN OVERVIEW

Harass: To disturb or irritate persistently; implies systematic persecution by besetting with annoyances, threats, or demands.[3]

Unfortunately, harassment is very familiar to students and to the school-based mediators who help them resolve conflicts. Most harassment is relatively innocuous but nevertheless hurtful and includes behaviors like teasing, name-calling, writing graffiti on bathroom walls, and spreading rumors. More serious forms—when one student consistently uses a racial slur against another, when a group of students silently move their lips to tease a student who is deaf, when a male student regularly touches a female student inappropriately—compromise the federally protected civil rights of young victims.[*]

Anecdotal evidence indicates that at least one quarter of the tens of thousands of conflicts mediated every year by school mediators involve some form of harassment. The purpose of this chapter is to consider when and in what form mediation is appropriate for these conflicts.

---

[*] Though the author hesitates to identify parties by a single characteristic, especially with such problematic terms as "victim" or "harasser," he sometimes does so in this chapter for ease and clarity of reading.

There is a surprising degree of subtlety involved in applying mediation to conflicts that involve harassment. To illustrate, let's first look at the issue of *adults* harassing *students* in school. One might assume that here at least, we could dispense with subtlety and quickly advise that such conflicts should not be mediated in primary or secondary schools. Such behavior, representing a serious abuse of adult responsibility, appears to necessitate an administrative and usually a punitive response.[*]

But conflicts between middle/high school teachers and their students are mediated regularly with great success. In a considerable portion of these conflicts, student parties claim that they have been "harassed" by the teacher. Perhaps they feel they are called on all the time, or it appears that the teacher holds them to different standards than their peers. For our purposes, whether students are perceiving these situations accurately is immaterial (though chances are that a good percentage of the time they are). When the case is appropriate, mediation has been effective and mediators are able to overcome the power difference between most students and adults relative to institutional authority, maturity, communication skills, and self-confidence.

Of course, mediation is not always suitable for adult-to-student harassment. Key here is to conduct a thorough intake interview. When it appears that the alleged harassment is real and serious, and especially when the alleged harassment impinges upon the civil rights of the student (sexual harassment, racial harassment, etc.), mediation is inappropriate as a first resort. All discussions with the parties, in private or face-to-face, should be conducted by an administrator who can then refer the conflict back to mediation if necessary.

Even if one were to prohibit the mediation of adult to student harassment, it would not make a big dent in the potential case load. Most harassment that students experience is carried out by their peers, often peers who are acquaintances and friends. Much of the time, both students (or groups of

---

[*] There had been considerable success using mediation to handle teacher harassment of students at the university level, but in these cases students are often adults or near adulthood.

students) are actively harassing one another. Wayne did X to Hee-Jin, which led Hee-Jin to do Y back, which angered Wayne so much that he did Z to Hee-Jin and her friends, and so forth. This is important, because when there is a relative balance between the parties as far as the harassment is concerned, it does not pose as significant a challenge to mediators. Such disputes can be successfully mediated using the standard process practiced by school-based mediators.

The real challenge for mediators occurs when this balance does not exist. For purposes of this chapter, "conflicts involving harassment" are defined as those in which the harassment is *not* reciprocal. There is either a clear victim and harasser, or enough imbalance between the severity of actions taken by the parties that an impartial observer would consider one much more responsible for the harassment than the other.

Why Mediation?

To understand mediation's strengths as a tool to help resolve conflicts that involve harassment, we must first review the alternatives. The most widely used intervention for incidents of harassment in schools is a punitive response from the disciplinary system. Administrators speak to the harasser after learning of the incident, punish him according to the severity of the actions taken, and possibly direct him to apologize to the victim in verbal or written form. In addition to internal school disciplinary channels, victims of harassment in the United States sometimes have the option of filing a complaint outside of the school system with the regional Office for Civil Rights. In the most serious cases, victims can also file suit in court against the school system and even individual students (or more accurately, students' guardians). Yet consider this example:

> It was upsetting enough that when Edgar received his math test
> back from Ms. Hooten, he saw that he got a D on it. But suddenly,
> Scott grabbed the test out of his hand and ran around the classroom
> shouting that Edgar was stupid. Edgar ran after him until Ms.
> Hooten stopped him and sent them both to the middle school office.

This is not a new problem for the boys. Scott is a bully, and he and his friends always pick on Edgar. They call him "bra strap," for instance, because he once wore a shirt that they thought looked like a bra. Scott even beat Edgar up one morning before school (for which the former was suspended). Now Edgar comes to school late just to avoid him. Edgar told his grandmother, with whom he lives, but she does not know how to help.

On their own, administrative punishment and lawsuits do not effectively resolve *interpersonal conflicts* between students who have an ongoing relationship. Scott had been suspended in the example above, but he continued to harass Edgar. Apart from the question of efficacy, the limitations of processes such as administrative hearings or lawsuits discourage victims from using them. These include:

THE REFORMATIVE EFFECT OF PUNISHMENT IS A BELIEF THAT DIES HARD, CHIEFLY, I THINK, BECAUSE IT IS SO SATISFYING TO OUR SADISTIC IMPULSES.

BERTRAND RUSSEL

—A focus on broken rules rather than broken relationships.[*]
—The process is quickly out of the control of the victim and in the hands of the authorities.
—Communication is primarily from parties to administrators; direct discussion between parties is not encouraged.
—The most formal processes are lengthy and public.
—Victims often do not want to get the harasser in trouble, something that usually results automatically from administrative processes.

Of course, punitive responses are sometimes necessary. Even lawsuits make sense for the most serious matters or when victims are unable to redress their grievances using other approaches. But when appropriate, mediation is a tool with many potential benefits:

• One of mediation's primary goals is to help parties truly understand (not necessarily agree with) each other's perspective. Mediators clarify misunderstanding and re-frame parties' statements to enable them to "hear" one another. The process also provides an opportu-

---

[*] Some feel that primarily focusing on rules leads students who harass to conclude that it is more important to avoid getting caught than to change their hurtful behavior.

nity for parties to do what they often desperately want: ask questions of one another (e.g., "What did you mean when you said that to me?" or "Why did you choose me to bother and not the other girls?") and make clear, assertive statements about what behavior is welcome or unwelcome. Even when victims are upset by the harasser's answers to their questions, they feel better about having answers rather than just questions.

- In mediation, the outcome and to a large extent the process remain in control of the parties themselves. This is something students often desire.

- A considerable percentage of harassment victims fundamentally want two things: first, for the offensive behavior to stop and second, to receive understanding and perhaps an apology from the harasser. They do not necessarily want the harasser to get in trouble or receive punishment. Many victims even hope to continue to carry on relationship with the harasser like it "used to be." For these parties, mediation is a welcome alternative to a strictly punitive approach.

- Mediation never precludes parties from using other avenues to address the situation, including initiating a formal disciplinary response before or after participating in the process. And the fact that students try mediation does not prevent the administration from delivering a clear message that certain behaviors are not acceptable: Students can receive disciplinary consequences *and* participate in a mediation session. In this way, mediation "is sensitive to the perspective and concerns of both parties" while also allowing for the school's need to control and eliminate harassment of all kinds.[4]

- Mediation emphasizes personal responsibility rather than external accountability, education rather than punishment. When conflicts change as a result of punishment—and too often they do not—it is usually only that the harasser stops engaging in the offensive behavior. But by confronting students who harass with the human consequences of their actions, underlying attitudes and values that led to the offensive behavior may be transformed. This depth of learning usually does not result from an exclusively disciplinary response to conflict resolution.

- Mediation provides the guarantee of confidentiality that is often desired by the victim (it is embarrassing to have been harassed) as well as by the harasser. Countless opportunities for effective intervention are lost in schools that primarily use public, administrative processes for addressing harassment.

- Because mediation is relatively quick, it can potentially bring the situation to a close soon after the parties request mediation services. This is what victims usually want most.

- Despite concerns about an imbalance in power between the harasser and the victim, mediation is often experienced by victims as an empowering process in which their voice is important, certainly as important as the harasser's. Mediation enables victims to be equals, have their views respected, and regain a feeling of control in their lives. Participants often achieve a clearer understanding of one another through mediation; this is as beneficial when parties do not share responsibility for the situation as when they do. (There is also no guarantee that the balance of power will be any better in a formal hearing or disciplinary procedure.)

The Challenge of Mediating Conflicts Involving Harassment

By their nature, conflicts involving harassment possess characteristics that test the boundaries of mediation and recommend important changes in its structure. These characteristics include:

1. **Mediators work in the shadow of the disciplinary system.** Most harassment that takes place between students contravenes their school's disciplinary code. This means that the conflict, especially the harasser, often must receive administrative attention. Administrative responses to harassment range from immediately involving legal authorities, in the most serious instances, to doing relatively little, to probably the most

common approach of combining punishment with an attempt to educate the harasser about their inappropriate behavior. If the parties try to mediate, it is usually certain that one or both of them has to return to the disciplinarian's office to discuss the situation. This disciplinary "shadow" falls over the mediation session and can affect the way parties behave.[5]

2. **The dispute is unbalanced.** In many mediation sessions, even if initially there appears to be a clear victim and harasser, both sides come to discover that they have acted in ways that have contributed to the conflict. But by our definition of "conflicts involving harassment," one party has behaved in a way that offended or injured a second and the latter has done little if anything to provoke the first. Give and take between parties who have co-created their problem is therefore not possible here. In addition, the harasser may have more actual or perceived power than the victim: physical power, institutional power, the support of peers, a facility with language or culture, cognitive ability, etc. This deepens the imbalance from the mediators' perspective.[*]

3. **Harassers may have less incentive to invest themselves in the mediation process.** Students who have harassed may be unwilling to participate in mediation. On the one hand, if they have met with administrators prior to their contact with mediators, they might feel pressured and not participate in good faith. On the other, if they receive punishment from the disciplinarian prior to mediation, they may feel they have nothing to gain from participating in the process. This is especially true when parties have no prior relationship or when there is nothing specific that the student who has harassed wants from the victim.

4. **The possibility of re-victimization exists.** In conflicts involving harassment there is always a concern that either the harasser or the mediation

---

[*] Compton and Paterson have noted that despite this dynamic, by the time parties come to mediation, often the harasser as well as the victim feel intimidated and powerless. The victim fears the harasser who has victimized her. The harasser fears both the victim's and the system's anger and demands.

process itself will re-traumatize the victim. This can happen in a number of ways. The necessity of discussing and to some extent reliving the victimization during a mediation session can upset the victim. The harasser's unrepentant words or behavior during a session—direct or subtle, intentional or not—can also make the situation worse for the victim. Finally, an angry, dissatisfied harasser might continue to bother the victim inside or outside of school after the mediation process has concluded. (It is important to note that the possibility of re-victimization is present, and perhaps more likely, when using a solely disciplinary approach as well.)

5. **There is a "past" orientation.** In mediation, parties generally discuss the past only to the extent that it is necessary to move them towards a satisfactory future. The dynamics of conflicts involving harassment make this more difficult, however. In these disputes, incidents and remarks from the past—and the parties' interpretations of those incidents—are of primary importance. Unlike with other issues, one party's offer to merely "not do it again" is usually insufficient to satisfy the other party. Victims usually also want a sincere apology from a harasser who understands and takes responsibility for his or her wrongdoing. To varying degrees, victims also want the person punished.

A Useful Model: Restorative Justice and Victim-Offender Mediation

One place to look for inspiration and instruction regarding mediating conflicts involving harassment is restorative justice and victim-offender mediation. This approach to justice and its related form of mediation address disputes that in many ways resemble conflicts involving harassment.

Restorative justice refers to an approach to justice and conflict resolution that contrasts with the more familiar institutional approach known as retributive justice. When someone wrongs another, retributive processes seek to assign blame and punish the offender. If someone breaks into a home, for instance, the criminal justice system (the most familiar retributive system) sets about trying to find, convict and punish the person responsible. The victim might testify in order to help convict the offender, but no opportunity is provided for dialogue between them. As in all retributive approaches, there is little focus on the specific needs of the victim or on the education of the offender. The punishment is also devised by neither victim nor offender but by the court. Most school disciplinary systems are essentially less formal versions of this retributive system.

In contrast, the philosophy of restorative justice asserts that when one person victimizes another, the victim, the community, and the offender are each harmed. The needs and concerns of the victim are paramount, but instead of asking who is guilty and how he can be punished, restorative approaches focus on healing and preventing a recurrence by repairing the harm done to all. This means, to the extent possible:

- helping victims restore their losses, answer their questions, calm their fears, and heal their wounds;
- helping communities create and participate in the enforcement of their norms and hold their members accountable; and
- helping offenders take responsibility for their actions, learn from their mistakes, right their wrongs, and reconcile with their victims.

ALL MEN MAKE MISTAKES. BUT A GOOD MAN YIELDS WHEN HE KNOWS HIS COURSE IS WRONG, AND REPAIRS THE EVIL.

All forms of community-based restorative justice operate as an adjunct to the punitive justice of the state. Victim-offender mediation, one such form, is also one of the fastest growing applications of community mediation. Here offenders and those they have victimized are brought face-to-face to discuss the offenders' crimes and attempt to repair the damage they caused. Currently almost 200 victim-offender programs exist in the United States and Canada. Many exclusively mediate crimes that involve juveniles or crimes to property, but the process is increasingly used to handle more serious offenses like rape, other violent assaults, and vehicular homicide.

The actual mediation process used by victim-offender mediators developed in response to the challenges of bringing such parties together. School mediators can apply lessons from this unique form when mediating conflicts that involve harassment, conflicts which have many similarities to victim-offender mediations. Four key aspects of the victim-offender mediation process are significantly different from the standard school-based approach:

1. **The offender must admit responsibility for wrongdoing prior to mediation.** The most striking difference between victim-offender and school-based mediation is that the offender must admit guilt and express a desire to make amends to the victim *before the mediation takes place*. The reality and absolute fact of their wrongdoing is not something that is negotiated. If the offender appears unwilling to take responsibility for the effect of their crime during preliminary meetings, the conflict is considered inappropriate for victim-offender mediation. This practice enables all participants to concentrate on healing rather than arguing over what happened in the past. Compare this to the typical school mediation session, in which the focus is on the subjective needs of the parties and where even broaching issues of right and wrong is discouraged.

2. **Mediators are "neutral" in a different way.** Following from the first difference, many victim-offender mediators have a distinct understanding of their impartiality. Like all mediators, they do not favor one party over another, they do not take sides, and they do not make judgments of right or wrong. But in this context, parties participate in the process as a victim and a offender, a wrongdoer and someone to whom a wrong has been done. The mediation session becomes a vehicle not just to help resolve a conflict, but also to help right a wrong. As such, although mediators hope their work benefits both victim and offender, they are not neutral as to the wrong.[6] Mediators acknowledge the harm done to the victim in order to facilitate the healing of all concerned.[*]

3. **Extensive preparation of parties by mediators prior to the face-to-face sessions.** Some victim-offender mediators spend a great deal of time in private meetings preparing (some even refer to it as "coaching") parties

prior to mediation. In part this is to establish the rapport and trust in the mediator that is essential in this highly charged context. Some of the topics addressed in these meetings—educating the parties about mediation, ensuring that they have realistic expectations, determining whether they want to mediate—are similar to what is covered in school-based intake interviews.[+] In order to prevent re-victimization and increase the chances of success, however, victim-offender mediators go well beyond the focus of the typical intake interview. Here they:

- help the offender consider the effects of the crime (and therefore the concerns of the victim) and how he or she might meaningfully compensate for the victim's losses
- help both parties practice expressing themselves in a way that will be most effective (using "I messages," for instance)
- ensure that both parties have the additional assistance (therapy, Alcoholics Anonymous, etc.) necessary for them to heal the wounds associated with the crime

Occasionally victim-offender mediators meet numerous times with each party in private, and even give them homework to complete in between meetings. In the most serious cases there may be as much as a year of preparation.

4. **Community participation in mediation sessions.** Operating with the assumption that a crime against an individual is also a crime against the community, some forms of victim-offender mediation include community members as participants. Both victim and offender can invite family members, friends, and advocates to support them through the mediation process. Other individuals who were affected by the crime directly or

---

* Acknowledging the harm done, without placing blame or guilt, is a challenge for some victim-offender mediators. Mediators might say something like the following: "The impetus for our being here is the recent incident in which the courts ruled that Mr. Victim was injured by Ms. Offender. Our goal today is to help you explore your thoughts and feelings about this situation in the hope that it will be beneficial to both of you."

+ In the school setting these interviews are primarily conducted by mediation coordinators, who arrange for parties to meet with mediators later if they choose to try the process.

who care about participants may also attend. The same careful screening is done with all participants to ensure the safety of parties and the potential success of the process. In typical school-based mediation, of course, it is rare to have participants other than the parties. Even parties' parents are usually discouraged from participating.

Informed by this brief review of victim-offender mediation, look again at the process of mediating conflicts involving harassment in schools. Although school mediators may not directly apply the insights gained from victim-offender mediation, they may find them applicable for managing the similar but less intense dynamics found in harassment disputes.*

Suggestions for Mediating Conflicts Involving Harassment

Taken together, characteristics of conflicts that involve harassment—the potential legal and disciplinary issues, the need to prevent re-victimization, and the power imbalances among parties—represent a very real challenge to mediators and warrant caution. Careful case screening and intake is essential to assess whether a dispute is appropriate for mediation. When one is, school mediators must maintain the integral principles of mediation (voluntariness, impartiality confidentiality, interpersonal transformation, self-determination and safety) at the same time that they support the institutional goal of eliminating harassment.

A Careful Intake

Of course, the issues involved in a potential mediation case are usually not clear prior to conducting an intake interview. Coordinators often learn only the rough details of the situation from referral sources, and some of this information may be inaccurate. When meeting for the first time with a student who has self-referred, coordinators may begin knowing absolutely nothing about the conflict. Initially, coordinators should proceed as they

---

* It is essential that school-based mediators receive additional training before mediating true victim-offender disputes.

would in all intake interviews: attempt to build trust, determine whether the case is appropriate for mediation, and encourage parties to try mediation if it is.[7]

Coordinators should always hesitate to draw conclusions about a case until after interviewing *both* parties. It may seem clear that the party in the first intake is the victim of harassment; that is, until one speaks with the supposed harasser, who makes similar claims. Sometimes both parties are right: each is harassing the other and is responsible for escalating tensions between them. But equally often it becomes clear that one party is primarily the *harasser*, and the other primarily the *victim*, regardless of what the harasser claims.

In these latter cases, which we have called "conflicts involving harassment," the first party to contact the coordinator will most often be the victim. Perhaps he or she came directly to the mediator for help, or the party may have been referred by an administrator, a teacher, or a friend. A helpful way to conceptualize the goals of intake interviews with victims of harassment is to provide three fundamentals during the process:

1. **Support.** It is difficult and sometimes dangerous to seek help when one is being harassed. Coordinators' first goal, therefore, must be to engender students' trust and demonstrate that mediation is safe and responsive. Build rapport by listening well, showing compassion for victims, and *never* blaming them. Coordinators can also refer victims to counselors, student groups (gay/straight alliances, diversity groups, etc.) or others in or outside of school who might provide support and help them cope with the effect of the harassment.

2. **Information.** Secondly, make sure that students are well informed concerning their rights and the available options for redressing their grievance. Familiarize victims with informal processes like mediation as well as with more formal procedures such as initiating a complaint within the school system or filing suit in court. Help them consider the relative

strengths and limitations of each option (e.g., it is difficult to win a case in court, and going to mediation does not guarantee that harassers will stop their behavior).

Mediation is an appropriate intervention only when both parties make an informed decision to participate. But being the primary provider of information to parties can strain a mediator's ability to be unbiased. Whenever possible, therefore, refer parties to others who can effectively and sensitively provide this information.

> Mediators must proceed with great caution when they help students who have been victimized gain assistance from school administrators and understand their rights. No longer only mediators, these individuals are now advocates as well. If mediation sessions do occur, mediators must be cognizant of how these actions affect their ability to be unbiased, both in reality and in the eyes of the parties.

3. **Choice.** Finally, after parties feel supported and are well informed, help them consider: What outcome do they wish for? What do they want and need in order to resolve the conflict? Apart from wanting the harassment to stop, do they want the harasser punished? Do they want to continue to have a relationship with them? Is keeping the incident confidential of great importance? Do they want to tell their parents what happened? Help parties clarify their needs rather than simply taking their responses at face value. Answering these types of questions will help parties determine their response to the basic question: Do they want to mediate?

It is essential that parties who have been victimized feel in control of the process of resolving their conflict. They should not be required to try non-adversarial processes prior to initiating formal disciplinary proceedings, and if they choose to mediate first, they should know that formal procedures are still available to them any time they choose.

Informing Administrators and Parents

The guarantee of confidentiality in mediation is one of the process's greatest strengths, and school-based mediators must always strive to preserve parties' rights to privacy. At the same time, however, both school administrators and parents have a legal right to be informed about certain kinds of behavior. It is also sometimes in student parties' best interests for administrators and parties' parents to know about a conflict. Mediators have to manage this challenging issue using knowledge of their rights and responsibilities, the school's disciplinary code, their ideally close working relationship with administrators, and their understanding of each conflict.[8]

By the time a conflict involving harassment comes to the attention of a coordinator or mediator, often school administrators already know about it. They may have even referred the parties to mediation. When administrators are not aware of the conflict, however, mediators must ask the victim and the harasser during the intake interview: Would they like the administration to know about the incident (and have their potential support and authority involved)? Many parties will want to seek assistance from the administration. If students are going to contact administrators on their own, follow up with them to make sure a formal complaint has been filed.

The severity of the harassment or other details of the conflict sometimes convince coordinators that the administration needs to be informed regardless of a party's wishes. Perhaps one student held a knife to the throat of a friend who did not pay for drugs, or a group of students continually taunts a boy who has a disability. In these cases, still attempt to solicit the parties' support. Many times the victim if not the harasser will agree to work together with the coordinator to decide how the information might be shared.[*] When the coordinator is skilled in these matters, it is relatively rare that he or she feels compelled to inform administrators against the wishes of the parties.

---

* It is not unusual for the coordinator or mediator to walk a student to the disciplinary office, introduce them to the disciplinarian, and help them inform administrators about the situation. Because documentation is helpful, parties might also draft a written version of events for submission to the disciplinarian.

On those few occasions when the coordinator feels that administrators need to be informed nevertheless, invite parties to present the situation to the administration anyway. Inform parties that there is still the possibility that administrators will allow them to mediate the case without taking disciplinary action, or mediate before or after such action.

The issue of informing parties' parents should be approached similarly. Coordinators and mediators help parties explore the reasons for and against this, and encourage students to inform their parent or legal guardian when appropriate. Defer to students' wishes and let them take the lead whenever possible.

When coordinators decide that parents need to be informed about a conflict involving harassment, this necessitates that the administration be informed as well. It is therefore always the *administration's* responsibility to contact parents in accordance with school policy. If mediation is still an appropriate intervention, administrators may then require that parents sign a waiver before giving students permission to participate in the process.

Whether students are going to inform parents on their own, or the administration feels obliged to do so in spite of students' wishes, be sure to offer continuing support to students. They may need help discussing the conflict with their parents.

Conducting Intake Interviews with the Student who has Harassed

If a student who has been victimized would like to try mediation, then someone needs to contact the other party, the student who has harassed. Before contacting the alleged harasser, it is essential to ask victims whether and in what manner they would like this to occur. Often this is a moot point: The harasser is aware of the conflict and of the fact that outsiders, from the mediation program or the school administration, are involved in the effort to resolve it. When the administration is involved, the manner and timing of contacting the harasser is usually out of the mediator's control.

But sometimes the harasser is not aware that a victim has sought help. In these cases, ask the victim how they would like to proceed. Can the coordinator contact the harasser? If the victim says no, explore their hesitation and attempt to calm their fears. Are they frightened of retaliation? Schools have strict prohibitions against retaliation (a discussion with the administration will make this clear). If the victim fears that the situation will become public and therefore even more embarrassing, inform them that mediation is confidential. If the victim hesitates to get the harasser in trouble, explain that mediation alone can result in disciplinary consequences only if the harasser agrees to them voluntarily. Help parties think through what will result if they take no action. This discussion will help coordinator and victim decide how to proceed. Of course, it is ultimately the victim's decision whether to mediate or not; barring their permission to contact the harasser, mediation cannot take place.

If the student who has been victimized does give the coordinator permission to contact the harasser, clarify whether the victim feels comfortable having the coordinator inform the harasser that the victim came to mediation for help. (Alternatively, coordinators can always try to avoid this issue when they speak with harassers.) Coordinators should invite the harasser to speak with them in private. To the extent possible, keep even the invitation confidential so that teachers and peers are not aware of it. Encourage the supposed harasser to speak as much as possible at the start of the interview; wait to explain the victim's concerns. Experienced coordinators report that often a harasser will say quite quickly: "I know why I am here....it's because of X, isn't it?" and proceed to explain his or her version of events.

A HATEFUL ACT IS THE TRANSFERENCE TO OTHERS OF THE DEGRADATION WE BEAR IN OURSELVES.
SIMONE WEIL

Taking a cue from victim-offender mediators, be sure to explore the extent to which harassers feel responsibility for their behavior. Do they blame the victim, or do they admit their guilt and want to make amends? Many stu-

Harassment Overview

dents will be contrite from the start, coming to this on their own or as a result of conversations with administrators.[*] Others' feelings of guilt and shame increase when they learn more about the impact of their behavior upon the victim. Be careful to leave the assigning of blame to the administration, however. As a coordinator, focus on building rapport with the student and determining the applicability of mediation to the conflict.

When introducing mediation to students who have harassed, make it clear that they are not exempt from disciplinary consequences if they participate in it. Even so, numerous aspects of the mediation process—the fact that it gives them an opportunity to explain themselves and learn how their actions affected the victim, that it is confidential, that it is quick—might convince them to try it. Of course, and as always, their participation should be completely voluntary.

Five Criteria For Deciding Whether Mediation Is Appropriate for Conflicts Involving Harassment

It was hard enough for Elaine to make friends and feel comfortable at school. She was recently "mainstreamed" back into her public high school after spending many years in a separate program for students with special needs. But two girls were really making things difficult.

Their names were Heather and Jacqui, and it seemed like they teased Elaine everywhere she went. Elaine was obese; she had struggled with her weight for as long as she could remember. Heather and Jacqui called her "fat pig" in the halls and in class. They wrote "oink" on her books. Every day when they were done eating their lunches, they dumped the leftover food from their trays onto Elaine's plate. It was humiliating for her.

Elaine tried to ignore this and fit in as best she could. She didn't know what else to do. One day, a nice boy encouraged Elaine to

---

[*] By formally assigning blame and enforcing consequences, school administrators can "inspire" students who harass to take a critical look at their behavior.

*tell the teacher about what Heather and Jacqui were doing, but
she didn't know how. Finally, a teacher saw Jacqui putting food
all over Elaine's clothes, and they were all sent to the office.*

During intake, mediation coordinators help parties understand the choices
they have for resolving their conflict. They explain the potential risks and
benefits of mediation, and parties ultimately decide whether they would like
to try the process. Apart from parties' decisions, however, coordinators and
mediators must decide whether they are willing to mediate a conflict that
involves harassment. Each case must be examined individually. Consider
the following five criteria to determine acceptability:

1. **The degree of harassment, including its severity, persistence and pattern.** Does it appear that the harasser acted
   maliciously, or was he unaware of or misjudged the consequences of his actions? The mildest cases will be very
   appropriate for mediation; the most egregious should be
   referred to the administration initially, with a mediation session possibly to follow. It is essential to stress, however, that
   *the seriousness of the harassment does not in and of itself make a
   conflict inappropriate for mediation.* If all other factors bode
   well (the victim is self-confident and after serious reflection
   truly wants to meet with the harasser, the harasser sincerely
   desires to make amends, etc.) then mediation may benefit
   parties to conflicts that involve even the most odious
   kinds of harassment.

2. **The victim's desired outcomes as expressed during the intake
   interview.** If he or she has a strong desire to speak with the
   harasser, then mediation might be appropriate. If he or she
   only wants the harasser to get into trouble, then directing the
   victim to utilize the disciplinary system would be advisable
   (even if the victim expresses an interest in mediation).

3. **The harasser's attitude towards trying to resolve and understand the conflict.** Does he take no responsibility for his behavior, or does he regret his actions and is eager to apologize? This is perhaps the trickiest criterion. Not always operating under the shadow of a powerful disciplinary system like victim-offender mediators, school-based mediation coordinators cannot be as categorical. Certainly mediators must guard against re-victimization; there is no reason to subject a victim to a harasser who is mean and unwilling to examine his or her behavior. But sometimes harassers who do not exhibit remorse initially are transformed by hearing the victim's full story during the mediation session.

4. **The victim's psychological strength, self-confidence, and ability to communicate needs verbally.** Does he or she have support outside of the session for confronting this difficult experience? Remain sensitive to students' age and ability to make decisions for themselves.

5. **The school's policy and procedures concerning the type of harassment in question.** Is the harasser likely to receive disciplinary consequences? If so, then it is wise to wait until after punishment has been assigned—the harasser may face suspension and not even be in school—before helping parties consider mediation.

Carefully review the specifics of the conflict when deciding whether mediation is appropriate for a harassment case. Though all factors may not be ideal, if on balance it appears that parties would benefit from participation in mediation, it is usually worth the associated risks.

To understand how to apply these criteria, let's return to the two conflicts presented in this chapter: one between Edgar and Scott (see page 43), the other involving Elaine, Heather and Jacqui. The mediation coordinator conducted intake interviews with all of the students. As far as Edgar and Scott's dispute was concerned, the coordinator learned that:

- The precipitating incident was not severe enough to necessitate a disciplinary response, but there was a history of problems between the boys.
- Though Edgar, the victim, was afraid of Scott, he was very articulate about his needs and concerns.
- Scott did not seem to understand how hurtful his behavior was to Edgar. He said he was just having fun. Though he did not say so directly, the coordinator also sensed that Scott was envious of Edgar's usually high academic performance.
- Although the parties were not friends, they were in three classes together and so had an ongoing relationship.
- Scott had already been suspended, but this had little effect upon his behavior towards Edgar.
- Edgar just wanted Scott to leave him alone.

After separate intake interviews with Elaine, Heather and Jacqui, the coordinator discovered that:

- Heather and Jacqui's behavior appeared to be malicious.
- Elaine was very afraid of the girls, especially of Heather.
- Elaine had a difficult time expressing herself verbally.
- Heather and Jacqui had no appreciation of the impact their behavior was having upon Elaine. They saw it all as a joke. The coordinator also knew from previous contact that Jacqui had tremendous psychological problems resulting from a difficult home life. She engaged in this kind of behavior regularly.
- The three girls had no classes together, were in different grades, and had no obvious reason to interact with each other.

As is the case in these disputes, the best decision is often not absolutely clear. In the first case, with both parties willing to mediate, the coordinator decided to schedule a mediation session. The results were fairly typical of school-based harassment cases: Scott agreed to leave Edgar alone, and the two decided to go their separate ways. Two weeks later, Edgar reported no further problems with Scott. The two were not friends, but they didn't seem to have difficulties anymore. Edgar also said during the follow-up interview that when he and Scott were assigned to work on a report together, he heard Scott say to a friend that he was happy he got paired with a "brain."

In the second case, though all of the parties were willing to mediate, the coordinator felt that it would be inappropriate to schedule a session. The main reason was Heather's and especially Jacqui's immaturity and apparent unwillingness to consider Elaine's perspective. It appeared that the two girls wanted to participate in mediation so they could *continue* to pick on Elaine, and the coordinator did not want to set the latter up to receive more abuse. (Although Elaine's limited communication skills presented another obstacle, the coordinator felt that this could have been managed had all other things been equal). Jacqui and Heather were sent to speak with the principal; Elaine was referred to a counselor for help.

There are steps that coordinators can take to change the balance in a case. Referring students to the administration prior to considering mediation might make parties more interested in the process. Encouraging a victim to meet with a counselor or student support group (gay/straight alliance, diversity committee, sexual harassment group, etc.) might enable him or her to be a more assertive and competent negotiator. In conflicts where there are multiple harassers and only one victim, having the victim mediate separately with each harasser (or with the key harassers) might be an effective strategy.

AFTER THE FINAL NO
THERE COMES A YES
AND ON THAT YES
THE FUTURE WORLD
DEPENDS.

WALLACE STEVENS

Two other interventions warrant attention: One mediation coordinator asks that parties write a letter to each other and bring their letter to a preliminary private meeting. She edits the letter with each party, taking out accusations and sarcasm and re-framing the language so that the other party will be more likely to understand. Then *the coordinator* presents the letters to each party in private and answers their questions as best she can.

Sometimes this process leads to a joint session in the end; sometimes it doesn't. In another mediation program, trained "victim surrogates" replace the real victims of harassment, and the *surrogates* "mediate" with harassers. The surrogates are trained to educate and inform rather than blame the harasser.

Mediator Selection

- **Provide advanced training to mediators.** The dynamics of conflicts involving harassment can fluster less experienced mediators. In addition to exploring the process modifications below, help mediators consider how to remain unbiased when there is a clear victim and harasser in the session.

- **Choose mediators wisely.** As in all challenging cases, be cautious when assigning mediators. Student mediators of all ages regularly mediate conflicts involving harassment in age-appropriate and ultimately effective ways. Experienced adults or adult/student teams should handle the most difficult cases. (Virtually all victim-offender mediation is conducted by adults). Mirroring the parties according to key characteristics (gender, sexual orientation, race, clique) is essential when these characteristics are related to the issues in conflict.

During the Session

Although characteristics of conflicts that involve harassment provide a unique challenge to mediators, as of this writing, most school-based mediators use their basic process, without modification, to handle these cases. Certainly there is no need to disregard what is working. But the more a dispute meets our definition of a "conflict involving harassment," with a clear victim and a harasser, the more mediators will find the following suggestions helpful. Simply reflecting upon the modifications outlined below should make mediators more sensitive to these conflicts.

Harassment Overview

- **Focus the session on "righting a wrong" rather than resolving a conflict.** When appropriate, shift the focus of the session from the typical exploration of all parties' role in co-creating a conflict to a focus on the injustice done by one to another. Practically speaking, instead of asking both parties to share their story of the conflict, mediators could offer the harasser the opportunity to explain his or her behavior and recognize its impact upon the victim. Or conversely, invite the victim to explain the impact of the harasser's behavior. Time devoted to creating an agreement instead becomes time for the harasser to propose a method of restitution and, if both parties desire, to reconcile. Be cautious, however, of condemning or shaming the harasser; strive to help the harasser as well.

- **Emphasize dialogue rather than agreement.** Key concerns of parties involved in harassment are usually what happened, why it happened, and how it affected them. Whenever possible, encourage parties to speak directly to each other. This can generate empathy and create a shared understanding of, if not what actually happened, then at least what each party experienced. One useful question to begin the dialogue, especially in situations where the harasser is not taking full responsibility for their actions, is: "If you could go back in time to a certain point in this dispute, where would you go and what would you do differently?"

- **Guard against re-victimization.** Mediators must be prepared to terminate the process whenever it appears to be reinforcing the victim's trauma. Be alert for cues like painful emotions that do not seem to be released, a sudden defensiveness or acquiescence from the victim, or a "harassing" quality to one party's behavior toward another.

- **Increase the use of private sessions.** Many mediators use private sessions more regularly in cases that involve harassment. This provides a safe place in which both parties can explore sensitive issues they otherwise might not divulge in a joint session. Even though it prevents parties from engaging in face-to-face discussion, sometimes parties' wishes and comfort levels necessitate that a large portion of mediation take place in private sessions with only a brief joint session.

• Allow parties to have an advocate accompany them during the process. In most applications of the mediation process in North America, especially in schools, parties are discouraged from bringing friends, witnesses or advocates. Mediators experienced in conflicts involving harassment, however, hold a unique view on this issue. Taking their cue from victim-offender mediation, these mediators understand that advocates and friends can deepen support for the process, balance the power, and provide information for parties. (Advocates, for instance, can suggest creative forms of restitution—writing an article, working to change school policy, reading a book—that parties might not have considered.) Some victims seek help only because of an advocate's support, and they would not feel comfortable in mediation without this person present. As long as these individuals understand their role and agree to abide by mediation's ground rules, support people can be crucial to a successful mediation.

No intervention will be appropriate for every conflict. When conducted judiciously by skilled mediators, however, mediation can have a profound effect upon parties to conflicts that involve harassment. By enabling parties to discuss their situation honestly and as equals, the process usually calms victims' fears and pushes harassers towards a greater understanding of the impact of their behavior. Though challenging, it is well worth the effort.

EVERY BLADE OF GRASS HAS ITS ANGEL THAT BENDS OVER IT AND WHISPERS, "GROW, GROW."

THE TALMUD

Resources

Books

Restorative Measures: Respecting Everyone's Ability to Resolve Problems
Minnesota Department of Children, Families and Learning
(651) 582-8454

Harassment Overview

Harassment Overview

Organizations

The Victim Offender Mediation Association
c/o The Restorative Justice Institute
PO Box 16301
Washington, DC 20041-6301
(703) 404-1246
web site: www.voma.org

Restorative Justice Initiative
Minnesota Department of Corrections
1450 Energy Park Drive, Suite 200
St. Paul, MN 55108-5219
(651) 642-0306

Center for Restorative Justice and Mediation
School of Social Work
University of Minnesota
386 McNeal Hall
1985 Buford Avenue
St. Paul, MN 55108
(612) 624-5888

Checklist
MEDIATING CONFLICTS INVOLVING HARASSMENT

INTAKE

✓ Provide (or make sure parties are provided with) three fundamentals (53):
- Support
- Information
- Choice

✓ Do not draw conclusions about a case until after speaking with *both* parties (53)

Conducting intake interviews with victims (52):

✓ Ask victims whether and in what manner they would like the harasser to be contacted

✓ If victims would not like the harasser contacted, explore their hesitation and attempt to calm their fears

✓ Remember: It is ultimately the victim's decision whether to mediate or not

Conducting intake interviews with harassers (56):

✓ If the victim would like the harasser contacted, invite the harasser to speak in private, keeping even the invitation confidential

✓ Ask open-ended questions at the start of the interview to encourage the harasser to speak; wait to explain the victim's concerns

✓ Build rapport with the harasser

✓ Explore the extent to which the harasser feels responsibility for his or her behavior (but leave the assigning of blame to the administration)

✓ Clarify that the harasser is not exempt from disciplinary consequences if he or she participates in mediation

Informing administrators and parents (55):

✓ Balance parties' rights to privacy with administrators' and parents' rights to be informed about certain kinds of behavior

✓ Ask the victim and the harasser whether they would like the administration and parents to know about the conflict

✓ Defer to parties' wishes whenever possible

✓ If administrators need to be informed despite parties' wishes, invite parties to present the situation to the administration nevertheless

✓ It is always the *administration's* responsibility to contact parents

✓ Offer to help students communicate with their parents

Five Criteria For Deciding Whether Mediation Is Appropriate For Conflicts Involving Harassment (58):

1. The degree of harassment (including its severity, persistence and pattern)

2. The victim's desired outcomes

3. The harasser's attitude toward trying to resolve and understand the conflict

4. The victim's psychological strength, self-confidence, and ability to communicate needs verbally

5. The school's policy and procedures

Coordinators can make a case more appropriate for mediation by (62):

✓ Referring students to the administration prior to mediation

✓ Encouraging victims to meet with a counselor or student support group

✓ Allowing parties (especially victims) to have an advocate accompany them during the process

✓ Having the victim mediate separately with the key individuals involved in a group conflict

✓ If, on balance, it appears that parties would benefit from participation in mediation, it is usually worth the associated risks

MEDIATOR SELECTION

✓ Provide advanced training to mediators (63)

✓ Use mediators who share key characteristics with, or "mirror," the parties (63)

✓ Choose experienced student and adult mediators (63)

DURING THE SESSION

✓ Focus the session on "righting a wrong" as well as resolving a conflict (64)

✓ Encourage parties to speak directly to one another when appropriate (64)

✓ Focus on facilitating dialogue more than formulating concrete agreements (64)

✓ Terminate the process whenever it appears to be reinforcing victims' traumas (64)

✓ Use private sessions when necessary (64)

3

MEDIATING CONFLICTS INVOLVING SEXUAL HARASSMENT

WRITTEN WITH DENISE MESSINA

Ramon began bothering Annette the very first day of middle school. She walked by him that morning—all kids had to pass where he and his friends stood waiting for the bell—and he whistled and said things. Annette couldn't hear what Ramon and the others said, but she was scared. She was in 6th grade; most of those kids were in 8th!

The next day, and the next, they did the same thing. They said comments about sex and about the way she dressed. Sometimes they talked loud enough so she could hear. One day, a boy named Howie said he wanted to "rip off her clothes." A mean girl named Laura added: "Howie, I didn't know you liked little babies."

Read Chapter Two for the fundamentals of mediating conflicts involving harassment.

For a long time Annette didn't mention this to anyone. She was increasingly nervous about walking to school, however. She didn't know whether the kids would really do something to her. Sometimes Annette asked her mom for a ride, but most days she had to walk. She tried to dress differently and walk to school at different times, but nothing helped. Eventually she told her mom, and her mom went to speak with the principal.

Sexual harassment has likely been with us for as long as there have been men and women. Untold numbers of women and girls (and to a much lesser extent men and boys) have had to endure this insidious form of discrimination, most with little personal and institutional support. Not until the 1991 spectacle of Anita Hill testifying about the behavior of Judge Clarence Thomas did this problem emerge full-blown into the collective American consciousness. The intervening years have witnessed a slowly increasing sensitivity to this issue.

The same problems found in North American society at large are present in its schools. Here too, sexual harassment had been primarily ignored or dismissed as "boys will be boys." Thankfully, many educators are now concerned about sexual harassment among students and between teachers and students.

Two recent studies indicate the extent of the problem. In one conducted by the Wellesley College Center for Research on Women, 39% of girls responding said they were sexually harassed on a daily basis.[9] A second study by the American Association of University Women surveyed 1600 male and female public school students in grades eight to eleven and found that:

- 80% of all students had been the victim of some form of sexual harassment, the overwhelming majority of which was student to student.[10]
- 32% of all students experience sexual harassment by 6th grade.
- 25% of females and 10% of males say they were harassed by school staff.
- 66% of males and 52% of females admit being perpetrators of sexual harassment.[11]

These startling numbers indicate that sexual harassment has a profound impact upon the educational experience of students, especially female students. In addition to the emotional turmoil that this violation engenders in young people—anger, embarrassment, self-consciousness, fear, lack of confidence and confusion—the effect upon their relationship to school is equally significant. These effects include not wanting to go to school, avoiding specific classes or hallways, getting lower grades, not wanting to be "visible" in class (and therefore decreased participation) and even dropping out. Thirty nine percent of female students and eight percent of male students expressed concern for safety in school due to sexual harassment.

A secondary problem is that victims often do not report sexual harassment. Only 7% of the students who had experienced harassment in schools actually told school personnel, and 23% told no one at all.[12] Unfortunately, there exists an intrinsic and powerful set of disincentives to reporting sexual harassment in schools, including:

—fear of being ostracized by peers

—the assumption that it does not happen to other students

—fear of retaliation

—not wanting to get the harasser in trouble

—fear that parents will discover previously hidden information about dating habits

—victims' confusion about whether they "asked for it"

Any approach to this problem is deficient unless it attempts to overcome these disincentives and encourage victims to take steps so that they no longer suffer in silence.

Sexual harassment is especially troubling in the school setting, where both victim and harasser are in the process of developing their character and understanding of the world. It is significant that the studies report that when boys sexually harass girls, they do so most often in public classrooms and hallways rather than in seclusion.[13] When not addressed appropriately, harassers and their impressionable peers may walk away from incidents of sexual harassment thinking that the behavior is acceptable. (All adult harassers were students once.) And victims who are unaware of their rights might tolerate harassment because they don't know that they have other options.

OF MY TWO "HANDICAPS," BEING FEMALE PUT MANY MORE OBSTACLES IN MY PATH THAN BEING BLACK.

SHIRLEY CHISHOLM

Sexual Harassment

Sexual harassment erodes students' legal rights, makes them feel unsafe in their own schools, and interferes with their education. Educators must address this issue in their buildings, creating considered and comprehensive approaches that teach young people early that sexual harassment will not be tolerated. Although more exploration is needed, mediation, done with skill, sensitivity and caution, should be an integral component of any approach.[*]

What is Sexual Harassment?

Mary, an 11th grade girl, was sitting in the cafeteria and drawing cartoons of naked people with her friends. Some 9th grade boys were sitting at the table next to them. One of the pictures fell at the feet of Wyatt, Mary's neighbor. When Wyatt picked it up and saw what was on it, he was really embarrassed. Mary said: "If you think that is bad, you should see this one," and she held up a picture of a girl with big breasts. Mary's friends laughed, and Wyatt and the other 9th graders got up and left.

The next day on the bus, Mary handed Wyatt another picture. It showed a naked boy with no penis under the heading "Invisible Penis Boy." A few other kids saw the picture and started to tease Wyatt. He didn't understand why Mary was picking on him. Later Wyatt's friends convinced him to tell his guidance counselor what Mary was doing.

* * * * *

With three weeks until the end of school and the weather turning hot, Elizabeth was feeling good. When she saw Seth walking towards her in the hall, however, she didn't like the way he looked. Seth had wanted to date her since they were freshmen, but Elizabeth had never reciprocated. Now he seemed drunk or something. Seth stopped in front of her, blocking her way and

---

[*] Virtually all of the writing on the use of mediation for conflicts that involve sexual harassment has concerned the work setting. The few school-related articles the authors could locate focused on faculty-student harassment in the university setting.

preventing her from moving. He asked if she wanted to go for a walk. Elizabeth said no, and demanded that Seth get out of her way. He refused, and then tried to kiss her, pinning her body against the locker with his own. Elizabeth struggled free by kicking him, ran into the nearest classroom, and asked for help.

In order to create a comprehensive response to sexual harassment at school, and to understand mediation's place in it, mediators must first understand exactly what sexual harassment is. Sexual harassment is formally defined as "unwelcome conduct with a sexual basis that is sufficiently severe, persistent or pervasive enough to limit a student's ability to participate in or benefit from the education program *or* that results in a hostile or intimidating educational environment."[14] From a legal perspective, sexual harassment is a form of "gender discrimination": actions that limit or deny a person or group opportunities, privileges, roles or rewards on the basis of gender. Courts in the United States recognize the following two forms of sexual harassment:

1. **Quid Pro Quo.** Quid pro quo—in Latin, "this for that"—is the most direct form of sexual harassment. It involves one person expressing or implying that benefits will be forthcoming in return for sexual favors, or conversely, that refusal of sexual advances will result in negative consequences for the victim. Quid pro quo need not be stated directly but only implied to be in effect: A teacher, for example, might imply that a student will receive a better grade (or not be cut from a team, or be exempt from a final exam, etc.) if she touches his genitals. Because quid pro quo usually happens in private, it is quite challenging to prove in court; it is often one person's word against another's. Quid pro quo most often occurs when there is a considerable power differential between harasser and target (i.e., staff to student). Although it can apply to student to student harassment, it is much less common than the second form of harassment.

2. **Hostile Educational Environment.** This type of harassment, distinct from the "this for that" quality of quid pro quo, refers to any *conduct by*

an individual or *activity in a school* which has the purpose or effect of creating a sexually intimidating, hostile or offensive educational environment. It includes unwelcome behavior of a sexual nature which prevents, impairs or substantially interferes with a student's academic performance, enjoyment of or interest in school, or general well being. Verbal, non-verbal, and physical behaviors like the following can all be forms of this type of harassment:

- telling dirty jokes
- verbal kidding of a sexual nature
- displaying sexually graphic pictures
- impeding or blocking movement for the purpose of making a sexual advance
- making suggestive or derogatory comments about a person's body, clothing, physical appearance, or sexual activity
- questioning a person about his or her private life
- making sexually suggestive sounds or gestures directed to or intended to be heard by the individual
- requesting sexual favors
- attempted or actual deliberate close physical contact (patting, pinching, brushing, hugging, touching, kissing, rubbing, etc.)

As this list makes clear, sexual harassment is not a simple, single thing. Behaviors range from relatively harmless forms of sexual harassment on one end (Mary's apparent immaturity leading her to offend and intimidate Wyatt with crude drawings) to sexual assault on the other (Seth's behavior toward Elizabeth). The severity of impact of various behaviors is not always obvious, however. Unwelcome letters, phone calls and notes are considered very severe by the courts when they are threatening, deliberate, and there is the possibility of escalation. And a single incident of sexual harassment, if it is sufficiently severe, can create a hostile educational environment for a student (for instance, an attempt to grab buttocks, breasts, or genitals).

Other fundamentals that are important to know about sexual harass-ment are:

—Although most harassment involves a male harasser and a female victim, sexual harassment can also be female to male, male to male, and female to female.

—From a legal perspective, the *intent* of the harasser is much less significant than the *impact* of their actions. Regardless of whether an alleged harasser intended to bully or demean a victim, if the victim can prove that he or she felt intimidated by the former's behavior—and if the court decides that a reasonable person of the same gender and age would feel similarly—it is legally harassment.

—Sexual harassment is distinguishable from mutual friendships, sexual attraction or flirtation because these latter behaviors involve choice and consent. Requesting a date in person or by phone, or giving a gift would not constitute sexual harassment unless these actions were repeated numerous times when it was clear that they were unwelcome.

—Sexual harassment is not the same as dating violence, in which one person in a dating relationship uses physical, emotional, or sexual abuse to gain power and control over their partner. Alarmingly, studies have found that between 12% and 35% of teenagers have experienced some form of violence (pushing, shoving, even hitting) in a dating relationship. Because of the unique dynamics of this type of abuse—students often confuse the abusive behaviors with love, the abuse can be cyclical, and it is difficult for victims to end even the most destructive relationships—it is necessary to create a separate, proactive effort to deal with this problem.

Why Sexual Harassment is Different

From the perspective of mediation, sexual harassment is similar in many ways to other forms of harassment. The characteristic that is the focus of this type of harassment—sexuality—is a part of every human being, and so it is perhaps more common. But even the legal system sees sexual harass-

Sexual Harassment

ment as similar to other forms of harassment, and most legal protections have resulted from analogizing to precedents related to these other types of harassment.

An impressive series of factors set sexual harassment apart and require that mediators take a uniquely sensitive approach, however. The first is that when we discuss sexual harassment, we approach one of the most emotional issues in our culture: sex. Most people agree that someone should not force themselves sexually upon another person. But individuals have powerful and often semi-conscious associations relative to sexuality. North American culture as a whole is very conflicted about sexuality, seemingly promiscuous on the surface (as demonstrated by the widespread use of sexual images to sell consumer goods) but deeply conservative and private underneath (as evidenced by the almost complete lack of open discussion about sex). There is certainly no broad consensus about the place of sex in our lives, especially the lives of our more vulnerable young people. This makes it difficult to address this issue in an objective manner.

Another complicating factor is that sexual harassment is in most cases the stepchild of sexism and the age-old oppression of women. The behavior now known as sexual harassment has been tolerated and often encouraged for centuries. People's approach to this issue may therefore be influenced by justifiable anger at a long history of oppression and denial of basic human rights to women and girls. This helps explain some advocates' motivation to put an end to sexual harassment using an exclusively punitive approach.

Third, innuendo, inference, context and perception are more central issues in sexual harassment than any other form of harassment. Although sometimes it is blatant and obvious, sexual harassment between students often results from actions that are interpreted differently by the parties. If the nature of the relationship, the time frame, or the setting is changed, even the apparent victim might interpret the behavior differently. As Gadlin writes, sexual harassment is often "defined more by a difference in how par-

ticular actions are understood than by the actions themselves."[15] Look at
the following example:

> Keyanna and Justin, both in 9th grade, have been friends for
> many years. Although they have never actually dated, Keyanna
> has always liked Justin. For the last couple of months they have
> been talking so much that she even felt like they were boyfriend
> and girlfriend. A couple of weeks ago, however, Keyanna
> learned that Justin was seeing another girl named Andrea. She
> didn't tell Justin she knew about Andrea; instead she just avoid-
> ed him as much as possible.
>
> Last week, Justin sat next to Keyanna in chemistry lab. He
> asked her what was wrong. When she didn't respond, he started
> fooling around like he always used to, with sexual jokes and the
> like. He said he could "go down on her and never get tired."
> This never used to bother Keyanna—in fact, she used to like it.
> But now Keyanna told Justin she wasn't interested, and he
> should take his little tool elsewhere. Actually, she muttered to
> herself, he already had.
>
> Then today Justin approached Keyanna again and started talk-
> ing the same way. This time it was in the hallway where other
> students could hear. When Justin joked that Keyanna should step
> into the men's room with him, she lost her temper and told him
> to fuck off. She immediately went to her counselor to report that
> Justin was sexually harassing her.
>
> The counselor, Ms. Locke, spent over an hour with Keyanna.
> Keyanna was clear that she didn't want Justin to tease her any-
> more; she wasn't sure she wanted to continue their friendship.
> After reviewing the ways she could proceed, Keyanna decided
> that she wanted to speak with Justin directly in a mediation ses-
> sion. (He didn't even know that she knew about Andrea!) She
> called the mediation coordinator on Ms. Locke's phone.

Sexual Harassment

NOT A SENTENCE OR A
WORD IS INDEPENDENT
OF THE CIRCUMSTANCES
UNDER WHICH IT IS
UTTERED.

ALFRED NORTH
WHITEHEAD

Sexual Harassment

In this conflict, language and behavior that was acceptable to Keyanna three weeks ago is now unacceptable because Justin is no longer considered a romantic partner. And what had been tolerable in private became too embarrassing when her peers could observe. Justin might not have intended to sexually harass Keyanna, however, and might assert that she used to participate in this kind of discussion and even liked it.

Keyanna and Justin's conflict is only one example. A student might complain of harassment when they are in the vicinity of offensive behavior but are not its target. Or victims might laugh at behavior out of fear or discomfort, unintentionally giving a harasser the wrong message.

Yet another unique aspect of sexual as opposed to other forms of harassment is the profound tendency of the mostly female victims to feel guilty and blame themselves for the situation. This is often matched on the part of the mostly male harassers by an unwillingness to be self-critical and accept responsibility for their behavior. This dynamic, vexing to mediators and advocates alike, is rarely as pronounced in other forms of harassment in schools (over race, sexual orientation, clique, etc.).

Complicating matters still further is that with student-student harassment, both the victim and harasser are young people who by their nature are experimenting with sexuality, sometimes awkwardly and inappropriately, often sincerely unaware of the consequences of their actions. Adolescents are just learning how to flirt, to tell someone they like them, to make a pass at someone they find attractive. Having absorbed countless inappropriate messages from popular culture, they try their best to negotiate this extremely powerful, emotionally and hormonally charged, and often completely new aspect of their lives. One indication of the extent of the confusion here is that many young harassers actually like the people they victimize; some even purport to "love" them.

Finally, young people have a culture and language of their own, and the adults charged with supervising them are not always facile with this culture.

When differences of race and class exist in addition to age, even more potential for misunderstanding exists between adults and students. Young people may be more comfortable talking about sex—even within earshot of their teachers—than the latter were when they were students, for instance. One educator has even postulated that young people see women as equal to men more than do most adults over 50; an older man's attitude that young women should not hear lascivious talk strikes many students as absurd and sexist. While it is important for educators to prohibit unacceptable behavior, adults need to be cautious of solely using their own frame of reference to interpret students' actions in these matters.

Addressing Sexual Harassment at School: Legal Guidelines

We will soon see that mediation is one effective method for resolving conflicts that involve sexual harassment. But educators who understand the frequency and severity of this problem (and who are aware of their responsibility and legal liability for this issue) know that it cannot be the only method. Schools must develop a comprehensive approach that *prevents* sexual harassment from occurring and *intervenes* when it does. A short detour will help us understand the legal context within which all approaches must operate.

In US schools, sexual harassment is prohibited by Title IX of the 1972 Education Amendments. Title IX is enforceable in any school (and its agents) which is the recipient of Federal financial assistance. Though the statute suggests that schools have a clearly stated sexual harassment policy for students as well as school employees, it *requires* that schools create and publish grievance procedures through which students can complain of alleged sex discrimination. Title IX regulations also mandate that schools designate and train a "Title IX Coordinator" to receive complaints of sexual harassment.

The Office for Civil Rights (OCR) of the US Department of Education is the agency responsible for the enforcement of Title IX. According to their guidelines, when a student files a complaint alleging peer harassment,

Sexual Harassment

schools must investigate and take effective, prompt and remedial action. OCR recommends the following two steps:

1. Determine whether sexual harassment has occurred, considering the nature of the information, the credibility of the source of the information, the seriousness of the allegations, whether there have been other complaints about the alleged harasser, and so on.

2. If it is determined that sexual harassment has or is occurring, take "reasonable, timely, and effective corrective action"[16] by:

   a. Ending the harassment by any or all of the following: warning the parties, taking disciplinary action based upon the severity and any record of prior incidents; directing the harasser to have no further contact with the victim; directing the harasser to apologize; providing counseling for the victim and the harasser.

   b. Taking corrective action for the victim. As an example, if the victim withdrew from a class, offer her the chance to take the class again. Some schools have even reimbursed a student victim for the cost of professional counseling.

   c. Taking steps to prevent further harassment of the particular parties involved and within the larger school community. This usually means training students and teachers about how to prevent and how to report sexual harassment.

When schools do not take the actions outlined above, OCR has held them accountable.*

Increasing numbers of US states have legislation or executive orders reiterating and expanding upon the OCR guidelines. At this time, the number of school sexual harassment cases (especially peer harassment) that have been actually litigated in the United States is small, but the law continues to

---

* Significantly, until June of 1998 schools were liable for sexual harassment whether or not they were aware of its occurrence: responsible not for the actions of the harassing individuals, but "for their own discrimination in permitting the harassment to continue once the school had notice of it." ("Notice" in this context means that the school knew about or should have known about the problem. USDE/OCR, p. 1.) Because the legal implications of this issue are increasingly serious, constantly shifting, and differ from state to state, it is important to consult with a local attorney when creating a policy.

evolve in this area.* In a landmark 1992 case known as Franklin v. Gwinnett County Public Schools (503 U.S. 60, 1992), the US Supreme Court decided that students may sue their schools for monetary damages associated with the incidence of sex discrimination. Since then, students have gone on to sue and force their school systems to pay monetary damages even for harassment conducted by peers.

As a civil offense in many localities, individual educators as well as their schools may be held personally liable for failure to protect students from sexual harassment. Mediation coordinators must be sure that their actions are consistent with their legal duty to use reasonable care and caution, both to prevent harm and in supervising and training student mediators. They should not let knowing more about the legal risks frighten them, however. As long as one follows some simple guidelines, uses common sense, and strives to do right by students, the legal risks associated with being a school-based mediator, or running a peer mediation program, are relatively small.[17]

Creating a Sexual Harassment Policy

Mediators should mediate sexual harassment cases only when their school's sexual harassment policy is effective and consistent with the legal requirements. An important first step towards mediating these conflicts, then, might be to improve a deficient policy. Use the following general principles as guides:

- **Give a clear message: Sexual harassment will not be tolerated!** All members of the school community should know that harassment of any kind, including sexual harassment, is unacceptable in school. No one should have to suffer this indignity. In addition to deterring students from engaging in harassment, this also conveys to victims that if they have the courage to come forward, their school will take them seriously and get them help.

---

* Most court decisions to date involve sexual harassment in the workplace and utilize Title VII of the Civil Rights Act (the employment related counterpart, and precursor to, Title IX of the Education Amendments).

- **Create an effective *punitive* approach to sexual harassment.** Related to the first point, the disciplinary system should be prepared to quickly respond to this behavior with outreach and support for victims, fair formal hearings, and widely understood and appropriately serious consequences. Develop consequences and process recommendations to match the severity of the harassment. Assertive disciplinary efforts only support mediation because the threat of punishment is a factor that can motivate parties to choose to participate.

  One popular disciplinary technique that integrates an educational component is letter writing. The victim writes a letter describing the behavior of the harasser, its effect upon her, and what she would like to happen. This letter is given to an administrator (not directly to the harasser), who arranges to meet with the harasser and formally presents him with the letter. At the bottom of the letter is a standard paragraph warning the alleged harasser about retaliation.

  Some schools devise creative disciplinary consequences for students who sexually harass. Students might be required to participate in a workshop on appreciating diversity, anger management, or sexism, for instance; some do relevant community service. Though mediation can be one part of the recommended process, there should "be no compulsion toward choosing mediation over other means of redressing a harassment grievance."[18]

- **Emphasize education.** As the National Organization for Women's Legal Defense and Education Fund's *Legal Resource Kit* states: "Laws against sexual harassment merely establish a minimum level of conduct for schools. The ultimate solution to ending harassment is prevention and teaching boys and girls to treat each other with respect."[19]

  Even though sexual harassment is a commonly discussed topic, it is frequently misunderstood. If adults talk in generalities ("sexual harassment is wrong!") and do not provide concrete examples, younger students may not understand which behaviors constitute sexual harassment. Whenever possible, educate students and adults concerning what sexual harassment is, why it is wrong, and how to get help if one is a target. This could include organizing in-service workshops for teachers, assembly programs supported by classroom lessons for students, and publishing the school's policy. One school used peer educators to co-facilitate workshops on sexual harassment. Another integrates discussion of sexual harassment into the social studies curriculum. When sexual harassment does occur, strive to teach victims how to protect themselves and harassers to see the negative impact of their behavior.

- **Be responsive to the needs of victims.** Regardless of the options available to redress this problem, ultimately the school must serve the needs of those who are harassed. Design a system that is quick, confidential, and that provides victims with a variety of formal and informal options according to their considered needs. In addition, given the reluctance of most targets to report incidents of sexual harassment, strive to make them as comfortable as possible and eliminate barriers to coming forward.

Mediation's Place in the Sexual Harassment Policy

> *When Noemi broke up with Steven last month, he was completely surprised, not to mention broken-hearted. The two had been going out for almost six months, and things were great as far as he could tell. They had lost their virginity together, a rite of passage for both of them. Noemi said she still wanted to be friends, but she just didn't feel the same way about him anymore.*

> *It wasn't until a couple of weeks later that Steven saw Noemi holding hands with Antoine, a guy who was a senior and a year older. His friends confirmed that the two were a couple. Noemi felt, he later learned, that Antoine understood her better and spent more time with her. This sent Steven into an angry funk that lasted for weeks.*

Then today in chemistry class, Steven started making references to how Noemi performed sexually. He said she "wanted it all the time." He spoke loud enough for half the class to hear, and he used glass tubes to illustrate sexual intercourse. Some guys started giggling. Noemi was outraged, and even though she told Steven to shut up, he just continued. After class she went directly to Mr. Rochester, the mediation coordinator and school counselor, to ask for help. He sent her next door to meet with the school's Title IX coordinator, Ms. Santos.

Ms. Santos was very nice; Noemi felt comfortable talking to her. Although at first she was extremely angry with Steven, Noemi eventually felt more sad than angry. After all that she and Steven had been through, she had really wanted to continue to be his friend. Or at least not enemies! Ms. Santos informed her about all of the different options she had, and Noemi said she wanted to think about it.

That night, Steven called but Noemi let the answering machine get it; she didn't want to speak with him. After a good night's sleep, and despite Antoine's insistence that __he__ take care of it, Noemi decided to try mediation. She told Mr. Rochester first thing that morning, and he agreed to contact Steven.

Steven was glad to learn from Mr. Rochester that Noemi wanted to speak with him. He felt badly about what had happened. He knew it was the wrong thing to do even when he was doing it, but he got carried away with anger. A mediation session was scheduled for the next day.

Steven and Noemi were full of feeling from the start of the session. Steven apologized immediately, but Noemi did not accept. She yelled, and then broke into tears, asking the mediators: "How could he do that?" Steven replied, also to the mediators: "I was wrong and all, but speaking of 'how could I do that,' she was the one who dumped me!" Noemi continued to cry, and no one spoke for what seemed like a long time.

Eventually, the two began speaking directly to one another. Steven described how jealous and hurt he was. Noemi explained that she broke up with Steven because he didn't give her the attention she wanted; he spent more time with his friends than with her. She stressed that it was not because of Antoine, who she got to know <u>after</u> they broke up.

In the end, Steven agreed to never bother Noemi. Noemi accepted his apology. They agreed to try to be friends again someday, but would go their separate ways for a while. Although there was a sad feeling at the close of the session, Noemi, Steven and the mediators felt they had done all they could for the moment. They would all have to see how things went.

Given sexual harassment's unique characteristics and schools' legal obligation to create a comprehensive policy to address it, how does mediation fit in? Can it be an effective tool to resolve conflicts that involve sexual harassment? When the harasser is an adult, and the victim a student in elementary, middle or high school, the answer is an unqualified *no*. An adult sexually harassing a student is too serious an abuse of power to warrant anything but administrative attention and punitive measures. In extraordinary cases, mediation could follow disciplinary action when administrators, mediators, students and their guardians determine that it would help.

But mediation is often appropriate for peer to peer sexual harassment, used either on its own or parallel with disciplinary action. Of course, mediation should not compromise the institutional message that sexual harassment is wrong and punishable. It should instead be used to educate, to facilitate clear communication, and to develop empathy and accountability in parties. In addition to the general strengths of mediation for harassment cases outlined in Chapter 2, mediation's unique strengths for sexual harassment cases include:

—Many cases of sexual harassment involve a significant discrepancy in the experience of the parties and a resulting lack of shared under-

Sexual Harassment

THE WEAK CAN NEVER FORGIVE. FORGIVENESS IS THE ATTRIBUTE OF THE STRONG.

MAHATMA GANDHI

Sexual Harassment

standing as to exactly what happened. With its emphasis on helping parties communicate effectively, mediation can be the perfect antidote. Students who have harassed especially gain from the opportunity to discover the error in judgment or perception that led to their behavior.

—When victims of sexual harassment have a history of trust and friendship with their harasser, they may be as confused and sad about the violation as they are angry. Mediation creates a safe setting for these parties to discuss their concerns and potentially heal their ailing relationship.

—Victims sometimes do not want their harasser to receive punishment. They just want the harassment to stop. For them, mediation is a welcome alternative to a strictly punitive approach.

—Few forums exist where young people, especially a male and female in conflict, can honestly discuss issues related to sexuality. Sometimes these issues must be broached in order to resolve conflicts involving sexual harassment. By putting students at ease and helping them articulate their thoughts and feelings, mediators enable parties to discuss such sensitive concerns.

—Incidents of sexual harassment can be full of ambiguity. As such, victims often do not have enough hard evidence to lead to a successful outcome in a formal hearing or legal proceeding. In mediation, however, they need little more than their feelings of discomfort to initiate a constructive dialogue with an alleged harasser.

Suggestions for Mediating Conflicts Involving Sexual Harassment

Consult Chapter 2 on mediating conflicts that involve harassment for general guidelines (page 52). Specific suggestions for conflicts involving sexual harassment follow below.

Intake

• To the extent possible, counter victims' tendency to blame themselves by asking concrete questions that expose erroneous assumptions ("Are you saying that because your dress was short, he had the right to make crude comments?").

- Be prepared to handle strong emotions when victims deal with the fear and embarrassment of being violated and harassers vent their anger or shame.

- Look for a cyclical nature to harassment between parties who have an on-going friendship or romantic relationship. If parties report an incident of harassment, then get along wonderfully, then report another incident, this is an indication that the harassment might approach dating abuse. In abusive relationships, the abuser may appear sincere and promise to change his behavior and make amends. But this sets the victim up to be abused again, and the severity of the abuse often increases until the cycle is broken. Refer the target (and if possible the abuser) to a community agency like a YWCA or domestic abuse hotline, where they can get the *independent* assistance, support, and counseling that they need. The unique dynamics of abuse usually make it inappropriate for mediation.

- If the school administration is or will be involved in the resolution of the conflict, consider having them "enforce" mediated agreements. A precedent for this unusual strategy exists at the college level, where harassers face suspension or even expulsion if they fail to live up to the agreement they help create in mediation. Discuss this practice at length with parties during intake to ensure that they understand and are willing to accept it as a condition of their participation in mediation.

- Many targets of sexual harassment will prefer not to mediate and meet face-to-face with their harasser. Remember that this is fine. In the conflict described on page 72, Elizabeth's disinterest in having any further contact with Seth was one of a number of factors that precluded their conflict from going to mediation.

- When parties want to mediate, review the five criteria discussed in Chapter 2 on page 58—the degree of harassment, the victim's desired outcomes, the harasser's attitude, the victim's psychological strength, and the school's policy—to determine whether the case is appropriate for mediation.

Title IX and Confidentiality

Maintaining confidentiality is an integral part of school mediators' work, but in sexual harassment cases, *all educators* must uphold a similar, rigorous standard regarding the privacy of information. The US Office for Civil Rights *Model Sexual Harassment Grievance Procedure* states explicitly that "allegations of sexual harassment shall be promptly addressed in a confidential manner so as to protect the privacy of all parties involved." If a victim (or victim's guardian) requests that the victim's identity or allegations be kept confidential, administrators must attempt to carry out an investigation—and when necessary, take steps to prevent other students from being harassed—without divulging this information.

Although the Office for Civil Rights currently supports informal methods of conflict resolution like mediation, it strongly prefers that the Title IX Coordinator be apprised of all incidents of sexual harassment. This represents a challenge to mediators who, along with parties, are usually free to decide who to inform about a conflict. One solution is to make the mediation coordinator the Title IX Officer. But this is not always possible.

When mediators and coordinators meet with victims, then, they should follow these steps:

1. Explain that: a) the Title IX Officer can most effectively educate harassment targets about their rights and options and b) that it is the Officer's responsibility to keep track of all incidents of sexual harassment in school. Make sure students understand that the Title IX Officer will strive to keep information confidential if they so request.
2. Ask victims whether they would be willing to inform the Title IX Officer about their conflict.
3. If parties refuse to speak with the Officer directly, ask if they would like the mediator to speak with the Officer on their behalf.
4. If parties prefer that mediators do not speak with the Officer, honor their wishes if at all possible. In those instances when the severity

of the harassment, the age of the students, the number of incidents, or the number of students involved warrant speaking with the Title IX Officer regardless of the victim's wishes, inform him or her of this as soon as possible.

Mediator Selection

- **Choose mature mediators.** Student mediators may handle these types of conflicts, but only those who can manage strong emotions and who are able to discuss sexuality in an age-appropriate way. When students do serve as mediators, most schools require that an adult be present in the room during the session. Otherwise, use adult mediators.

Suggestions for Mediators

Most of the strategies for modifying the mediation process for conflicts involving sexual harassment are listed in Chapter 2. One additional consideration follows:

- **Mediators, as coordinators, should be aware that victims are often quick to blame themselves, and harassers are just as quick to blame the victim.** One of the best ways to manage this dynamic—which has as much to do with male and female socialization as it does with sexual harassment—is to "reality test": "Do you really think that what you said to him caused his reaction?" "Were there many other girls dressed the same as you were today?" etc.

Federal laws, disciplinary codes, even mediation—none of these is *the* answer to the problem of sexual harassment. But given the pervasiveness of its cousin, domestic violence (the largest number of calls to many police departments is for domestic violence), we must do everything we can to help young people learn to treat each other with respect. Used with sensitivity, and with the voluntary participation of informed parties, mediation can help students embroiled in these conflicts take control of their lives, redress their mistakes, and move forward.

Sexual Harassment

Resources

Books

Sexual Harassment: It's Not Academic
US Department of Education, Office for Civil Rights
600 Independence Avenue, SW
Washington, DC, 20202-1100
(800) 421-3481

Flirting or Hurting?: A Teacher's Guide on Student-to-Student Sexual Harassment in Schools
Nan Stein and Lisa Sjostrom (Washington DC: National Education Association and Wellesley College Center for Research on Women, 1994).

Sexual Harassment and Teens
Susan Strauss with Pamela Espeland
Free Spirit Publishing, Inc.
400 First Avenue North, Suite 616
Minneapolis, MN 55401
(612) 338-2068.

Organizations

National Education Association
Human and Civil Rights Division
1201 16th Street, NW
Washington, DC 20036
(202) 822-7700

Programs for Educational Opportunity
University of Michigan
1005 School of Education Building
610 East University
Ann Arbor, MI 48109-1259
(734) 763-9910

NOW Legal Defense and Education Fund
395 Hudson Street
New York, NY 10014
(212) 925-6635

Center for Research on Women
Wellesley College
106 Central Street
Wellesley, MA 02481-8259
(781) 283-2510

Checklist
MEDIATING CONFLICTS INVOLVING SEXUAL HARASSMENT

INTAKE

✓ Provide (or make sure parties are provided with) three fundamentals (53):
- Support
- Information
- Choice

✓ Do not draw conclusions about a case until after speaking with *both* parties (53)

✓ Be prepared to handle strong emotions when victims deal with the fear and embarrassment of being violated and harassers vent their anger or shame (87)

✓ Look for a cyclical nature to harassment between parties that would indicate dating abuse (and inappropriateness for mediation) (87)

✓ If parties are willing, consider having school administrators "enforce" mediated agreements (87)

Conducting intake interviews with victims (52):

✓ Counter victims' tendency to blame themselves by asking concrete questions that expose erroneous assumptions (78/86)

✓ Ask victims whether and in what manner they would like the harasser to be contacted

✓ If victims would not like the harasser contacted, explore their hesitation and attempt to calm their fears

✓ Remember: It is ultimately the victim's decision whether to mediate or not

Conducting intake interviews with harassers (56):

✓ If the victim would like the harasser contacted, invite the harasser to speak in private, keeping even the invitation confidential

✓ Ask open-ended questions at the start of the interview to encourage the harasser to speak; wait to explain the victim's concerns

✓ Build rapport with the harasser

✓ Explore the extent to which the harasser feels responsibility for his or her behavior (but leave the assigning of blame to the administration)

✓ Clarify that the harasser is not exempt from disciplinary conse-

Sexual Harassment

quences if he or she participates in mediation

Informing administrators and parents (55):

- ✓ Balance parties' rights to privacy with administrators' and parents' rights to be informed about certain kinds of behavior
- ✓ Ask the victim and the harasser whether they would like the administration and parents to know about the conflict
- ✓ Defer to parties' wishes whenever possible
- ✓ If administrators need to be informed despite parties' wishes, invite parties to present the situation to the administration nevertheless
- ✓ It is always the *administration's* responsibility to contact parents
- ✓ Offer to help students communicate with their parents

In U.S. schools, it is preferable that the Title IX Coordinator be apprised of all incidents of sexual harassment. Approach parties as follows (88):

- ✓ Explain the role of the Title IX Officer
- ✓ Ask victims whether they would be willing to inform the Title IX Officer about their conflict
- ✓ If parties refuse to speak with the Officer directly, ask if they would like the coordinator to speak with the Officer on their behalf
- ✓ If parties prefer that the coordinator does not speak with the Officer, honor their wishes if possible
- ✓ When the severity of the harassment, the age of the students, the number of incidents, or the number of students involved warrant speaking with the Title IX Officer regardless of the victim's wishes, inform him or her of this as soon as possible

---

Five Criteria For Deciding Whether Mediation Is Appropriate For Conflicts Involving Harassment (58):

1. The degree of harassment (including its severity, persistence and pattern)

2. The victim's desired outcomes

3. The harasser's attitude toward trying to resolve and understand the conflict

4. The victim's psychological strength, self-confidence, and ability to communicate needs verbally

5. The school's policy and procedures

Sexual Harassment

Coordinators can make a case more appropriate for mediation by (62):

- ✓ Referring students to the administration prior to mediation
- ✓ Encouraging a victim to meet with a counselor or student support group
- ✓ Allowing parties (especially victims) to have an advocate accompany them during the process
- ✓ Having the victim mediate separately with the key individuals involved in a group conflict
- ✓ If, on balance, it appears that parties would benefit from participation in mediation, it is usually worth the associated risks

MEDIATOR SELECTION

- ✓ Provide advanced training to mediators (63)
- ✓ Choose mediators who (89)
  - Can manage strong emotions
  - Are able to discuss sexuality in an age-appropriate way
- ✓ Use mediators who share key characteristics with, or "mirror," the parties (63)

DURING THE SESSION

- ✓ Focus the session on "righting a wrong" as well as resolving a conflict (64)
- ✓ Encourage parties to speak directly to one another when appropriate (64)
- ✓ Focus on facilitating dialogue more than formulating concrete agreements (64)
- ✓ Terminate the process whenever it appears to be reinforcing victims' traumas (64)
- ✓ Use private sessions when necessary (64)

MEDIATING CONFLICTS INVOLVING HOMOPHOBIA AND SEXUAL ORIENTATION HARASSMENT

WRITTEN WITH BERNADETTE MURPHY

Read Chapter Two for the fundamentals of mediating conflicts involving harassment.

It seemed to Marcos like everyone hated him at the Rosa Parks Middle School. A few months ago this kid Bernard beat him up, and right after that a bunch of boys surrounded him in the alley across from school and would have hit him if an adult hadn't come. Those boys were suspended, but they still tease him. And now all the kids in his eighth grade class call him "gay" and "faggot" whenever they see him.

This truly disturbs Marcos. He can't concentrate in school anymore, and even if he knows the answer he won't raise his hand because he might be teased. Usually a quiet person, Marcos has also begun to verbally lash back at the students who harass him. Today, during math class, Theresa said that Marcos "has sex with Greg." Greg, who has special needs, was a neighbor and friend of Marcos' family. Marcos lost his temper and knocked Theresa's desk over. Both Marcos and Theresa were suspended.

When they returned to school, Theresa and all her friends continued to bother Marcos (even though she had promised the vice principal she wouldn't!). Marcos' parents spoke to the principal, Ms. Green, but she was unresponsive and said that by suspending the students who harass Marcos, she was doing all she could. Halfway through the year, Marcos and his parents decided that he should leave the Parks School and begin attending the other middle school in town.

This conflict illustrates a form of suffering that far too many students endure. Harassment based on sexual orientation is ubiquitous in North American schools. Despite tremendous gains in public tolerance and even appreciation of people who are gay or lesbian over the last three decades, the problem persists.

Homophobia—the irrational fear and hatred of people who are gay or lesbian—is the root of sexual orientation harassment. Not all conflicts that involve homophobia lead to sexual orientation harassment, however. Students may come into conflict over other issues and use homophobic language only when their tempers flare. Sometimes homophobia is clearly evident to mediators but is not of concern to any of the parties.

Sexual orientation harassment slightly different than its closest relative, sexual harassment. The latter is *harassment based upon gender* and is prohibited in US schools by Federal law (Title IX) and sometimes State laws. Sexual orientation harassment is *harassment based upon someone's actual or perceived sexual orientation*. Though currently not prohibited by federal laws, a small but increasing number of states (Massachusetts, Wisconsin, Connecticut) have amended existing laws that prohibit discrimination in schools on basis of race and gender to include sexual orientation. Some behavior would be considered both sexual and sexual orientation harassment.[*]

> IT IS A GREAT SHOCK AT THE AGE OF FIVE OR SIX TO FIND THAT IN A WORLD OF GARY COOPERS, YOU ARE THE INDIAN.
>
> JAMES BALDWIN

Homophobia

---

[*] Beware that the law in this area is constantly evolving. As this book was going to press, the US Supreme Court was about to rule on a workplace case that involved same sex sexual harassment.

One does not have to be among the estimated 7.2 million people under age 20 who are gay to be the victim of sexual orientation harassment.[20] All students, gay or straight, are potential targets and may receive the same treatment as an openly gay student. In fact, odds are that victims are straight more often than they are gay. Most students who harass, like those who bothered Marcos, don't even know the sexual orientation of their victim. In a very concrete way, then, making schools safe for gay and lesbian students makes them safer for everyone.

A Sexual Orientation Glossary

Bisexual: A man or woman who is attracted to members of either gender.

Dyke: A derogatory term for lesbian, sometimes appropriated and used with pride by same.

Faggot: A derogatory term for a gay man. Comes from the Middle Ages when the Christian church killed men suspected of being gay by laying them upon burning "faggots" (kindling wood). Some gays proudly reclaim this term as a sign of solidarity with their martyred brothers.

Gay: A synonym for homosexual, used by both homosexuals and lesbians to identify their sexual orientation.

Heterosexual: A man or woman whose feelings of romantic and sexual attraction are for someone of the opposite gender.

Homophobia: The fear and/or hatred of gays and lesbians; can be expressed in hateful language and many other discriminatory and hurtful behaviors.

Homosexual: A person whose feelings of romantic and sexual attraction are for someone of the same gender. Because this is a cold, "scientific sounding" term, most gays and lesbians do not use it.

Lesbian: A woman whose feelings of romantic and sexual attraction are for other women.

Out (also "coming out" or "being out"): A phrase used in the gay and lesbian community that refers to the state of being open or "out" about one's sexual orientation. Also refers to the process in which individuals stop hiding their sexual orientation and fully acknowledge it to

Homophobia

themselves and others. This usually involves accepting/celebrating one's sexual orientation and telling friends and family. Originally came from the phrase "coming out of the closet."

Pink Triangle: A symbol generally associated with the gay community. From an identity badge gay men were required to wear in Nazi Germany (an estimated quarter million gay men were killed in Nazi death camps).

Queer: A derogatory term for gays and lesbians, sometimes appropriated and used with pride, as in the organization Queer Nation.

Sexual Orientation: One component of sexuality, distinguished by an enduring emotional, romantic or sexual attraction to individuals of a particular gender. Sexual orientation is different than sexual behavior because it refers to feelings and self-concept.

Straight: A synonym for heterosexual. A person whose feelings of romantic and sexual attraction are for people of the opposite gender.

Transgender: A term with different and evolving meanings. It was first used to refer to individuals who surgically changed their gender. It is now often used to refer to individuals who feel their gender is ambiguous, who feel androgynous, or who experience themselves in a profound sense as being "of the opposite gender."

Why Sexual Orientation Harassment is of Special Concern

Homophobia is one form of prejudice, a subject which was discussed in Chapter 1. And the dynamics of Marcos' story resemble the conflicts involving harassment explored in Chapter 2. But four aspects of sexual orientation and the harassment related to it warrant the special attention of mediators.

- **Sexual orientation can be invisible.** While students easily observe who is African-American among them, they usually cannot see who is gay. Unlike skin color, gender and other physical qualities, sexual orientation is an invisible characteristic. Many corollaries follow from this fact, some of which can be problematic for those interested in eradicating this form of prejudice.

—People who are gay and lesbian often have the ability to hide their sexual orientation from even their closest friends and family members.

—Few students have the experience of working with a teacher whom *they know is gay*, despite odds that most students have actually had such a teacher. This is true of all the people in students' lives: They cannot identify the gay police officers, neighbors, shop owners, relatives, entertainment figures, etc.

—Many students, teachers, administrators, and parents assume that there are no gay or lesbian students in their schools.

—Both gay and straight students can be the target of vicious harassment on the basis of a presumed homosexual orientation.

- **Prejudice against gays and lesbians is the norm.** Homophobia is one of the most widely held forms of prejudice in North America today. The majority of public institutions, including many religious denominations, explicitly or implicitly discriminate against people who are gay and lesbian. And sadly, attitudes among educators are often not very different:

  —80% of prospective teachers and nearly two-thirds of guidance counselors expressed negative feelings towards homosexuality and about lesbian and gay men in a study conducted by the South Carolina Guidance Counselors Association.[21]

  —More than half of the students involved in 12 Massachusetts gaystraight alliances reported hearing teachers use homophobic language at school.[22]

Irrational and extremely hurtful myths about homosexuals (that they prey on young people for sex; that their presence encourages young people to "turn gay"; that they actively "recruit" students to their "lifestyle") are prevalent. Even non-homophobic educators, fearing for their jobs, can feel compelled to act in a way that panders to the prejudice in their communities. As a result, it is only in exceptional schools that gay and lesbian educators feel comfortable being "out" with their colleagues, much less with students.

HOMOSEXUALITY IS ALWAYS ELSEWHERE BECAUSE IT IS EVERYWHERE.

RENAUD CAMUS

Homophobia

- **Prejudice against gays and lesbians is rampantly applied.** Because homophobia is widespread, and because gay people can be invisible, few other prejudices are so freely acted upon in schools. Homophobic comments ("You dyke!" "That is gay!" "Are you queer?") are extremely common among students, in most cases running second only to "you're stupid" as the most used put-down. Students and adults are openly malicious towards gay people in schools without experiencing the routine public humiliation that would follow declarations of most other forms of prejudice. It is no accident that 86% of students report that they would be "very upset" if called gay or lesbian, and males identify being called "gay" as the most disturbing form of harassment.[23]

- **There is little support at home.** Hostility towards gays and lesbians does not end at the school yard: it exists at home as well. This sets it apart from most other forms of prejudice and harassment in schools. If a student is harassed for being a Jehovah's Witness or Asian or tall or speaking with a lisp, that student can usually count on finding support from his or her parents. The most significant cultural characteristics may even be shared by members of victims' families and wider community. But most gay and lesbian students cannot take comfort in the arms of loving parents or guardians. Half of all lesbian and gay youths interviewed in a 1987 study reported that their parents rejected them for being gay, and one quarter were actually forced to leave home because of conflicts with their families.[24] And so the harassment at school is compounded by a lack of understanding and possible harassment at home.

The climate in most North American schools and communities, then, is typified by ignorance and antipathy concerning homosexuality. This creates a destructive cycle of repression: Gay and lesbian adults and students do not feel safe identifying themselves ("coming out") in school; teachers and students conclude that there are no gay people in their community and continue to act out of ignorance. There is little opportunity for personal contact between gay and straight people that could educate everyone and potentially eradicate this prejudice.

And what of the adolescents who are coming of age sexually? Despite many parents' wishes that it were not the case, most students come to an initial understanding of their sexuality during their middle and high school years. This is difficult terrain for almost all students, gay or straight. Living in an environment filled with hostility, however, puts gay students in an especially precarious situation. Many live with the fear or reality of constant humiliation, discrimination and physical harm. They are overwhelmingly isolated because there appears to be no safe place to reach out for help. They become depressed, self-hating, and self destructive. The statistics speak for themselves:

—Almost half of gay males (45%) and one quarter (20%) of lesbians experience physical or verbal assault in high school.[25]

—69% of gay males report a history of school problems related to sexual identity, and significant numbers of gay and lesbian students feel forced to drop out of school due to harassment based on sexual orientation.[26]

—Tragically, lesbian and gay youths are two to three times more likely to attempt suicide than their heterosexual peers, and account for up to 30% of all completed suicides among youths.[27]

A Comprehensive Approach

To address this disturbing situation and eradicate homophobia in their schools, educators must create a comprehensive approach. The first step is to acknowledge that there is in fact a problem. For too many years, school administrators' silence on this issue directly contributed to the hostile climate in many buildings. The courage and commitment of all educators, straight and gay, is required to dispel homophobic stereotypes and make schools safe.

The mediation process is effective only as one part of a comprehensive effort to eliminate homophobia in a school: If used in isolation, and if the school environment is hostile towards gays and lesbians, mediation's impact will be greatly limited. Mediators sometimes take the lead in helping their

TO ME, REALIZING I WAS GAY WAS ALMOST LIKE BEING TOLD I HAD CANCER AT THE TIME. I THOUGHT: "MY GOD, HERE I AM SLIPPING AWAY FROM MY FAMILY, MY SOCIETY; I'M GOING TO BE INVISIBLE." I FELT A PHYSICAL SENSATION OF BEING ON A SHIP, AND THE SHIP WAS LEAVING FROM THE DOCK AND EVERYONE WAS STANDING ON THE DOCK AND THE SHIP WAS MOVING, AND I COULD DO NOTHING TO GET OFF THAT SHIP, AND THE STRETCH OF WATER WAS GETTING WIDER AND WIDER BETWEEN US.

ANDREW HOLLERAN

Homophobia

schools address this issue holistically. Focus on the following three areas:

1. **Develop a Policy.** Every school should protect students from sexual orientation harassment by officially prohibiting discrimination on the basis sexual orientation. Consequences for homophobic behavior should be appropriately severe and stated explicitly in the student handbook. Mediating conflicts that involve homophobia can be one option available through the policy.

2. **Educate the School Community.** Many people have a profound deficit in their knowledge about gays and lesbians. Often learning basic information about homosexuality dispels the pervasive mythology that surrounds it. Although addressing this issue directly is currently unrealistic for many communities, there will be increased opportunities for this educational work in the years ahead. Use credible and effective presenters, both adults and students, to develop empathy in participants for the struggle of fellow human beings. Teachers can participate in in-service workshops, students can learn in health or social studies classes, and parents can attend community meetings. Presentations may include personal stories, statistics, a review of the school's disciplinary policy, and suggestions to help participants intervene to stop harassment.

This work can be challenging. Many people harbor deep seated fears about homosexuality, while others sincerely believe that homosexuality is wrong or sinful. People can be hurt if they are encouraged to "come out" by a short-lived program that is followed by great opposition within the community. Evaluate the school climate carefully and gain the support of the school leadership before beginning such educational efforts. And approach the work using a theme—safety, suicide prevention, violence prevention, appreciation of diversity—that is important to the targeted audience.

3. **Provide Support.** Teachers, students and parents require ongoing sup-

port to educate themselves about sexual orientation as well as to manage the emotional concerns that this subject engenders. School counselors should be trained to be comfortable with all issues related to sexual orientation. In addition, many high schools and colleges form Gay-Straight Alliances (GSA's). These school-based support groups, pioneered in Massachusetts, provide students with a safe place to meet and discuss issues related to sexual orientation. GSA's also organize educational programs. The mere existence of a Gay-Straight Alliance in a school can make it a safer place for many students.

Suggestions for Mediating Conflicts that Involve Sexual Orientation Harassment

Linda, a sophomore, was hanging posters for her school's Gay-Straight Alliance when she noticed Eddie following her and writing on them. She walked over and saw he had written "Dykes and fags suck" in red marker across every one. Not someone to take this sort of thing lightly, Linda asked him: "What the fuck are you doing!?" He replied that the posters spoke for themselves and turned to leave. Linda tried to grab the marker out of Eddie's hands, and the two struggled briefly before a teacher separated them and escorted them to the office.

The assistant principal, Mr. Goldiers, spoke with each student privately. He explained to Eddie how serious his actions were: Not only had he defaced public property, he had violated the rights of a fellow student. He gave him five days detention. Mr. Goldiers empathized with how upset Linda was, but he said he was disappointed that she had started a physical confrontation with Eddie. He encouraged both students to meet with the school counselor, Mr. Fox, and consider having him mediate their dispute. After a brief meeting with Mr. Fox, both Linda and Eddie agreed to try mediation.

Linda was belligerent at the start of their session, and Mr. Fox

Homophobia

had to intervene to stop her from calling Eddie names. She said she was a lesbian, and she could not tolerate people like Eddie. Eddie said little, and his eyes rarely rose off the floor when he spoke. In a private session, however, Eddie explained that he didn't have anything against Linda in particular, he and his friends just didn't like gay people. Eddie mentioned that his step-father also criticized all the gay people on television.

When Mr. Fox brought them back together in a joint session, Linda and Eddie spoke calmly to each other for the first time. It turned out they were friendly with some of the same people. After much discussion, Eddie offered her an apology. He was unwilling to put up new posters for all those he had defaced (which was what Linda said she wanted), but Eddie was willing to never bother the posters again. Linda accepted his apology and gave an impassioned speech about accepting gay people. She also invited Eddie to come to the next GSA meeting, adding that "it is not called gay/straight alliance for nothing."

Months afterward, having seen each other many times at parties and in the halls, Eddie approached Linda in the cafeteria and gave her the red marker.

Mediation is an effective tool to help resolve conflicts that involve homophobia and sexual orientation harassment. The fundamental advice for intake and mediation of these cases is covered in the chapters on prejudice and harassment. In addition, consider the following suggestions.

Intake

With conflicts that involve any form of harassment, coordinators should carefully determine the acceptability of each case for mediation using the criteria introduced on page 59: the degree of harassment, the victim's desired outcome and psychological strength, the harasser's attitude, and the school's policy. One additional factor used to gauge acceptability with sexual orientation harassment cases is how comfortable parties are discussing the issue of sexual orientation. Remember: Coordinators and mediators may not know whether one or more of the parties is gay, and as a rule, they should not put parties on the spot by asking. This complicates matters. Parties who are harassed may or may not be gay; they may not know whether they are gay; and if they do know, they may not be willing or able to be open about this fact. The party accused of harassment might even be gay and hate him/her self because of this.

Rather than make assumptions about parties' sexual orientation, it is important to get a general sense of their ability to discuss the issue. This is especially true of the alleged victim. If that party is timid or unable to discuss this issue, then he or she might be vulnerable to further attacks and it may not be advisable to proceed with mediation. Refer these students to counselors for emotional support and to disciplinarians for protection from harassment. On the other hand, a victim who is comfortable articulating his or her feelings about sexual orientation might benefit greatly from the mediation process. Other specific factors to consider include:

- the kind of support parties have or are willing to accept at school and at home
- the balance of power between the parties (for example, if the victim is gay but not "out," the harasser's taunts and other behaviors are all the more powerful and potentially damaging)

Coordinators should take these factors into consideration—and when appropriate discuss them with the parties—as they help them decide whether to mediate.

Mediator Selection

- **Mirror the parties.** As in all conflicts that involve prejudice, strive to create a mediation team that "mirrors" key characteristics of the parties. Here that might mean including a co-mediator that is openly gay or lesbian and one who is straight. Mediators who are "out" must be able to accept parties who choose not to be out (as well as those who are not even ready to acknowledge to themselves that they are gay).

Homophobia

- **Use sensitive mediators.** Make sure mediators are comfortable discussing issues related to sexual orientation. Provide training so that all mediators know the language and "labels" acceptable to the gay community. (In addition to the glossary above, many gay advocacy and educational groups can help with this.) "Sexual orientation," for instance, is preferable to "sexual preference" because the former connotes an immutable way of being rather than a mere "preference." Student mediators who are comfortable with this issue *can* conduct these sessions effectively. (Young people may be more accepting of their homosexual peers than are many adults.) Also consider using community-based mediators when appropriate.

I BELIEVE ALL AMERICANS WHO BELIEVE IN FREEDOM, TOLERANCE AND HUMAN RIGHTS HAVE A RESPONSIBILITY TO OPPOSE BIGOTRY AND PREJUDICE BASED ON SEXUAL ORIENTATION.

CORETTA SCOTT KING

Suggestions for Mediators

- **Emphasize trust and safety.** Knowledge of a person's sexual orientation, in the wrong hands, can create life altering problems. A profound level of trust is therefore essential if parties, especially gay or lesbian parties, are to feel safe in mediation. Mediators build and nurture parties' confidence in them and in the process whenever possible by listening sensitively, giving parties control, highlighting confidentiality, setting a pace that matches parties' needs, utilizing private sessions, and so forth.

Mediation played an integral role in helping Eddie and Linda resolve their differences. But it was not used in isolation. The disciplinary system was quick to respond to Eddie's inappropriate behavior, and their school had already encouraged the formation of a Gay/Straight Alliance to support gay and lesbian students like Linda. Surely it will take many years to transform the climate in schools to one in which gay and lesbian students feel safe and appreciated. But used wisely, mediation can in a small yet significant way help to bring about this change.

Homophobia

Resources

Organizations

Gay, Lesbian, Straight Education Network (GLSEN)
121 West 27th Street, Suite 804
New York, NY 10001
(212) 727-0135; fax: (212) 727-0254
web site: www.glsen.org

Parents, Families, and Friends of Lesbians and Gays, Inc. (PFLAG)
1101 14th Street, NW, Suite 1030
Washington, DC 20005
(202) 638-4200; fax: (202) 638-0243
email: info@pflag.org
web site: www.pflag.org

National Gay and Lesbian Youth Hotline
(800) 347-TEEN
Hours: 7-10 p.m. (eastern standard time), Friday and Saturday evenings.

National Gay and Lesbian Task Force
2320 17th Street, NW
Washington, DC 20009-2702
(202) 332-6483; fax: (202) 332-0207
tty: (202) 332-6219
web site: www.ngltf.org

National Youth Advocacy Coalition
1711 Connecticut Avenue, NW, Suite 206
Washington, DC 20009-1139
(202) 319-7596; fax: (202) 319-7365
email: NYouthAC@aol.com

Human Rights Campaign
web site: www.hrcusa.org

Queer Resources Directory
web site: www.qrd.org

Homophobia

Checklist
Mediating Conflicts Involving Homophobia and Sexual Orientation Harassment

INTAKE

✓ Provide (or make sure parties are provided with) three fundamentals (53):
- Support
- Information
- Choice

✓ Do not draw conclusions about a case until after speaking with *both* parties (53)

✓ Be prepared to handle strong emotions when victims deal with the fear and embarrassment of being violated and harassers vent their anger or shame (87)

✓ Rather than put parties on the spot by asking about their sexual orientation, get a general sense of parties' ability to discuss the issue (104)

✓ If parties are willing, consider having school administrators "enforce" mediated agreements (87)

Conducting intake interviews with victims (52):

✓ Counter victims' tendency to blame themselves by asking concrete questions that expose erroneous assumptions (78/86)

✓ Ask victims whether and in what manner they would like the harasser to be contacted

✓ If victims would not like the harasser contacted, explore their hesitation and attempt to calm their fears

✓ Remember: It is ultimately the victim's decision whether to mediate or not

Conducting intake interviews with harassers (56):

✓ If the victim would like the harasser contacted, invite the harasser to speak in private, keeping even the invitation confidential

✓ Ask open-ended questions at the start of the interview to encourage the harasser to speak; wait to explain the victim's concerns

✓ Build rapport with the harasser

✓ Explore the extent to which the harasser feels responsibility for his or her behavior (but leave the assigning of blame to the administration)

Homophobia

✓ Clarify that the harasser is not exempt from disciplinary consequences if he or she participates in mediation

Informing administrators and parents (55):

✓ Balance parties' rights to privacy with administrators' and parents' rights to be informed about certain kinds of behavior

✓ Ask the victim and the harasser whether they would like the administration and parents to know about the conflict

✓ Defer to parties' wishes whenever possible

✓ If administrators need to be informed despite parties' wishes, invite parties to present the situation to the administration nevertheless

✓ It is always the *administration's* responsibility to contact parents

✓ Offer to help students communicate with their parents

Six Criteria For Deciding Whether Mediation Is Appropriate For Conflicts Involving Sexual Orientation Harassment (58):

1. The degree of harassment (including its severity, persistence and pattern)

2. The victim's desired outcomes

3. The harasser's attitude toward trying to resolve and understand the conflict

4. The victim's psychological strength, self-confidence, and ability to communicate needs verbally

5. The school's policy and procedures

6. The parties' level of comfort discussing the issue of sexual orientation, since victims who are timid or unable to discuss this issue might be vulnerable to further attacks and it may therefore be inadvisable to proceed with mediation (104)

Coordinators can make a case more appropriate for mediation by (62):

✓ Referring students to the administration prior to mediation

✓ Encouraging a victim to meet with a counselor or student support group

✓ Allowing parties (especially victims) to have an advocate accompany them during the process

✓ Having the victim mediate separately with the key individuals

Homophobia

involved in a group conflict

✓ If, on balance, it appears that parties would benefit from participation in mediation, it is usually worth the associated risks

MEDIATOR SELECTION

✓ Provide advanced training to mediators (63)

✓ Choose mediators who (89):
  • Can manage strong emotions
  • Are able to discuss sexuality and sexual orientation in an age-appropriate way
  • Share key characteristics with, or "mirror," the parties (63)

✓ Consider using community-based mediators when appropriate (106)

DURING THE SESSION

✓ Emphasize trust and safety because of the highly personal nature of these conflicts (106)

✓ Focus the session on "righting a wrong" as well as resolving a conflict (64)

✓ Encourage parties to speak directly to one another when appropriate (64)

✓ Focus on facilitating dialogue more than formulating concrete agreements (64)

✓ Terminate the process whenever it appears to be reinforcing victims' traumas (64)

✓ Use private sessions when necessary (64)

Homophobia

5

MEDIATING
ACROSS CULTURES

A change is taking place in the way in which North Americans see themselves. The long-standing metaphor of the region as a "melting pot," with its diverse peoples combining to create a single national character, is being replaced. Many North Americans now see the population more as a quilt, with each distinctive culture intact but woven into a somewhat harmonious whole. This new metaphor acknowledges that the undeniable differences among citizens cannot be subsumed into a homogenized mono-culture. It also respects the unique contribution that all people make to what it means to be North American. In short, North Americans have begun to appreciate their cultural diversity.

"Culture" refers to the expectations, institutions, beliefs, and practices that people create to understand and cope with their world. Cultures are shared among groups of people, and the "rules" of culture are taught both explicitly and implicitly to new members and children. These rules prescribe everything from religious practice to language to norms of human interaction to style of dress. Cultures appear to be static, but in fact they develop and change as a result of a gradual and never-ending dialogue between humans and their environment.

Because culture evolves in response to a particular place and time, the most comprehensive cultural systems are associated with national origin: We refer to Kenyan, British, Japanese, French, or Costa Rican culture. But there are many other categories by which we can delineate cultures, and these factors overlay the foundation of geographical origin. Cultures differ along religious, racial, and ethnic lines: A Catholic African-American, a Jewish European American, and a Buddhist Asian American, though they may live within ten miles of each other, have different cultural backgrounds. Among the many other variables that have an undeniable influence upon or are influenced by culture are social class, gender, sexual orientation, and generation. Even organizations like schools each have their own institutional "culture."

One outgrowth of North America's growing appreciation of its cultural diversity is a desire to re-examine institutions and their practices in this light. This is especially necessary in public institutions like schools, where in some communities Caucasian Americans of European ancestry are fast becoming the minority. It is increasingly important that both the substance and the process of education support students from all backgrounds. Students who are taught to appreciate their culture are more likely to appreciate themselves. And when young people appreciate themselves—when they have self-esteem—they make better school citizens.

To date, school-based mediation has been used successfully with parties from across the gamut of cultural backgrounds. But the mediation process must be similarly scrutinized regarding its applicability for the diverse population in North American schools. One thing is certain: Mediation as it is most often practiced here is a product of late twentieth century, North American culture. As such, the process has elements that are inappropriate or even offensive to parties from particular cultural backgrounds. These elements include not only simple procedural matters, but fundamental principles at the core of the process.

Prior to describing some examples, it is important to stress one point. Culture is learned by osmosis: by watching and internalizing how those around us behave. If one's parents disagree by arguing loudly and expressively, and if most of the people in one's community do the same, then an individual assumes that all people behave this way. To other people in other places, this method of expressing disagreement might appear unseemly if not insane! But it is all that one knows. Culture-bound behavior arises from assumptions that are semi-conscious and difficult to articulate. Approaching the subject of differing cultural behaviors and norms, therefore, presents a singular challenge: It forces us to suspend judgment and question ideas implicitly assumed to be true.

The following examples illustrate how various aspects of the North American mediation process might be inappropriate in other cultural contexts:

- The mediation process rests upon the belief that direct and open communication between parties in conflict leads to mutually beneficial resolutions. Many Asian cultures do not share this belief. Rather than directly confronting another party, people with this heritage may prefer to employ indirect methods to resolve conflicts (using an intermediary without face-to-face contact, ignoring the conflict, making a joke, etc.). Maintaining harmony—and sometimes only the *appearance* of harmony—is preferable to direct confrontation in which parties "lose face."

- Mediators strive to treat parties as equals, regardless of their age, their sex, their position, or their social class. In Latino and other cultures, however, respect for elders is a paramount value. A party of Puerto Rican descent might feel uncomfortable if mediators were younger than himself. And a teacher born in the Dominican Republic might find it offensive to mediate a conflict with a student twenty years her junior.

- In part because of the Western civilization's faith in science, we assume that people who are strangers to the parties and their conflict make the most effective mediators. The rationale is that strangers are more capable of maintaining their objectivity and impartiality. In many cultures, however, when people in conflict need help, they seek assistance from someone they respect and trust: the head of the household, an uncle or an aunt, an experienced community member

DIFFERENCES CHALLENGE ASSUMPTIONS.

ANNE WILSON SCHAEF

Culture

or religious leader. The concept of discussing private conflicts with complete strangers strikes many peoples as absurd.

- North American mediators usually help parties fashion agreements that are ultimately written down. This is because of a cultural assumption that written contracts signify a greater commitment than verbal agreements. This assumption is not shared by countless other cultures. For the Basques of Spain, for instance, "giving one's word" represents the highest degree of commitment. And for many Native Americans, written agreements carry the blemish of the hundreds of broken treaties throughout their history. Parties from these cultures might perceive mediators' preference for creating a written record of what has already been verbally agreed upon as insulting.

- Mediation emphasizes the power of the individual to control their own fate. Parties determine the resolution of their own conflicts in the privacy of the mediation session. In many cultures, however, the individual does not operate in such an autonomous universe. Instead, they have a clear and profound responsibility to their community. Parties' friends, relatives, and neighbors all have a stake in the outcome of their dispute. When the mediation process is used in these cultures, a community representative or elder either mediates or sits in on the sessions.

- Most mediators are taught that an essential aspect of listening is to look parties in the eye while communicating with them; making "eye contact" is a sign of respect and attentiveness in North America. In Cambodian and other Asian cultures, however, direct eye contact can be perceived as rude, prying or disrespectful. This is especially true if it is done by "inappropriate" people and at "inappropriate" times. Mediators who are simply making "eye contact" with Asian-American parties might be offending them unawares.

These are only a few examples of the tension between assumptions embedded in the mediation process and the beliefs of other cultures. The crucial task here is to determine how this tension affects mediation in North

Culture

American schools. Will individuals from particular cultural backgrounds feel uncomfortable taking advantage of their schools' mediation services? Are mediators unwittingly offending parties when they mediate, or misinterpreting their actions and words? Most fundamentally, is it necessary to modify the mediation process utilized in North American schools to make it culturally appropriate?

The answer to all these questions, especially the last, is a tentative yes: "Yes" because of course educators must work to make mediation effective for people of all cultures and backgrounds; "tentative" because to date the modifications that have been necessary have been relatively minor. Three reasons, taken together, explain why school-based mediation has been effective with *young people* from diverse backgrounds.

1. **Some behaviors—caring for children, utilizing tools and language, engaging in rituals—are inherently human.** They are practiced by people regardless of the particular culture within which they live. Mediating, broadly speaking, falls within this category. Although the form may differ, people helping other people resolve their conflicts seems to be universal human behavior.

2. **Mediation is fundamentally concerned with making parties comfortable and winning their trust.** An essential part of a mediator's work is to adjust the process when necessary to meet parties' unique needs. Although this does not guarantee that the process will be culturally relevant, it predisposes mediators toward being sensitive to concerns of this nature in practice as well as theory.

3. **Mediation efforts in North American schools primarily work with young people.** With the exception of recent immigrants, most of these students, although possibly born of non-American parents, are "bi-cultural:" They have an understanding of and a facility with Western customs and culture in addition to their first culture.*

> I REMEMBER ONE NIGHT AT MUZDALIFAH...I LAY AWAKE AMID SLEEPING MUSLIM BROTHERS AND I LEARNED THAT PILGRIMS FROM EVERY LAND—EVERY COLOR AND CLASS AND RANK—ALL SNORED IN THE SAME LANGUAGE.
>
> MALCOLM X

---

* The same is not true for adults. People who spend the first twenty years of their lives outside of North America—including many students' parents—often never gain proficiency with American language and culture.

Culture

Suggestions for Making Mediation Culturally Sensitive

The three factors above combine to minimize the cultural dissonance that young people might otherwise experience in mediation. Nevertheless, it is important to modify the process so that it is responsive to the needs of all potential parties. Take these steps to increase a mediation effort's sensitivity to culture:

In General

- **Be mindful of the impact of culture upon parties' experience of mediation.** People who mediate in schools, and especially those who implement peer mediation programs, are pioneers. As such, it is necessary to maintain an open mind and an ever-inquisitive attitude. The most problematic aspects of the mediation process as far as cultural sensitivity is concerned are the implicit and unquestioned assumptions upon which mediation operates. Keep notes on one's experiences, interview parties before and after sessions, study program's records, experiment with alternative approaches, and share experiences with others in the field.

- **Become familiar with the specific cultures with which one is likely to work.** This is a daunting task in schools where over twenty cultural backgrounds are represented, but in many schools there is a predominance of students from two to five cultural backgrounds. Read about these cultures and develop trusting relationships with students and their families. These efforts will provide insights regarding what is and is not appropriate for various cultures. Then modify the mediation process as needed to suit the norms of specific cultural or ethnic groups.

Do not assume, however, that a party is predisposed to specific norms solely because they were born into a particular culture or race. People with similar heritage can differ widely both in their facility with the dominant culture as well as in the degree to which they personally identify with their heritage. A Chinese-American party, for instance, might be as

Culture

"American" in outlook and behavior as any other US citizen. Approach each person as a unique individual.

Mediator Selection

- **Integrate information about cultural differences into peer mediation training.** Include training on culture as part of the mediation training, either the initial training if time permits, or during advanced training of mediators. Both "culture-general" and "culture-specific" training should be included. The former helps trainees explore their own cultures and potential biases and understand the impact of culture generally. The latter concerns teaching mediators about specific cultures and how they might work with them. Cultural training can be presented by mediation trainers, by a coordinator, and/or by guests speakers. This training makes mediators more effective and enables them to encourage student parties to appreciate their cultural heritage. Beware of allowing culture-specific knowledge to lead to stereotyping, however. Mediators should use this training as a tool to help them understand, not completely define, potential parties.

- **Train a culturally diverse group of peer mediators.** One of the strengths of the peer mediation concept is its utilization of a diverse pool of student mediators. These mediators also become primary resources for information about the cultures that are represented in the school. Their insights make it possible to change the mediation process so that it serves the school community most effectively. Equally important, a diverse pool of mediators provides the program with the ability to assign mediators who will understand the cultural dynamics of a conflict.

During the Session

- **Alter the mediation process to accommodate parties' cultural needs.** Because there is no universal intercultural conflict resolution method, each dispute much be approached individually. To date, mediators report altering the process in the following ways:
  - —During their opening remarks, mediators acknowledge that miscommunications may result from the differing cultural expectations of

Culture

the participants. They apologize in advance for any mistakes they might make and encourage parties to voice their concerns and ask questions if they are uncomfortable.

—Throughout the process, mediators strive to explain the rationale behind their actions. For example, instead of summarizing what parties say as a matter of course, a mediator might explain: "Now I would like to summarize what you have just said. This is to ensure that I have understood you correctly, as well as to let you know that you have accurately represented your concerns."

—Mediators work predominantly and sometimes exclusively in private sessions, enabling them to test their process assumptions and allowing parties to save face.

—Mediators minimize eye contact and paraphrasing of parties' needs and feelings.

—Verbal rather than written agreements result.

—Adult mediators, or adult-student teams, are utilized rather than only student mediators.

—Coordinators include, with parties' permission, parents, community leaders or elders in mediation sessions. (This strategy and the one that follows are usually appropriate only when parties share the same cultural background.)

—Mediation sessions are conducted in parties' homes or places of worship instead of at school.

—Mediation sessions are conducted in a party's first language that is not English.*

—Parties are allowed to choose mediators they want to work with rather than having a coordinator assign the mediators.

The relationship between cultural assumptions and the mediation process is one of the most subtle and fascinating aspects of this work. There may be times, due to specific culture-related issues, when it appears that mediating a

AN UNLEARNED CARPENTER OF MY ACQUAINTANCE ONCE SAID IN MY HEARING: "THERE IS VERY LITTLE DIFFERENCE BETWEEN ONE MAN AND ANOTHER, BUT WHAT THERE IS IS *VERY IMPORTANT*."

WILLIAM JAMES

Culture

---

* See Chapter 10 for information on how to use interpreters effectively.

dispute is inappropriate. This is fine. With care and attentiveness, however, mediation can be a highly effective process for parties from most every cultural background.

Resources

Books

Conflict Resolution Across Cultures: From Talking It Out to Third Party Mediation
Barbara Filner and Selma Myers
Amherst Educational Publishing, PO Box 6000
Amherst, MA 01004
(800) 865-5549

Organizations

National Association for Multicultural Education
University of Wisconsin at Madison
Department of Curriculum and Instruction
Teacher Education Building
225 North Mills Street
Madison, WI 53706
(608) 263-4601
Publishes a magazine on multicultural education and is committed to inclusion and cultural pluralism

Culture

Checklist
MEDIATING ACROSS CULTURES

IN GENERAL

✓ Remain aware of the implicit assumptions about human behavior upon which mediation operates (112)

✓ Become familiar with the specific cultures with which you are likely to work (116)

INTAKE

✓ Be mindful of the impact of parties' culture upon their experience of mediation (116)

✓ Do not assume that a party is predisposed to specific norms solely because they were born into a particular culture or race (116)

MEDIATOR SELECTION

✓ Integrate information about cultural differences into advanced mediation training (117)

✓ Train a culturally diverse group of peer mediators who can serve as a primary resource for information about the cultures represented in the school (117)

✓ Select mediators who will understand the unique cultural dynamics of each conflict (117)

DURING THE SESSION

✓ Beware of allowing culture-specific knowledge to lead to stereotyping (117)

✓ Apologize to parties in advance for mistakes that might result from insensitivity or ignorance of their cultural norms (118)

✓ Encourage parties to voice their concerns and ask questions when they are uncomfortable (118)

✓ Explain the rationale behind your actions whenever possible (118)

✓ Alter the mediation process to accommodate parties' cultural needs (117)

✓ Be alert to any discomfort in parties that might be attributable to cultural factors (115)

Culture

6

MEDIATING
CONFLICTS
BETWEEN
STUDENTS AND
TEACHERS

Lucia, a 7th grade student, felt that her teacher, Ms. Reardon, always favored other kids. The most recent example had to do with their book reports. Ms. Reardon told Lucia's friend Ivy that she only had to read two chapters for the report, but she told Lucia that she had to read her entire book.

Ms. Reardon also yells at Lucia all the time and sends her to the office. Whenever she mentions Lucia's parents, Ms. Reardon says: "I am going to have to speak with your father!" Lucia doesn't like this because it makes it seem like she doesn't have a mother.

For her part, Ms. Reardon has had difficulty with Lucia since she was "included" into her class at the start of the year. Lucia has serious learning disabilities and works much more slowly than her peers. She also has a terrible temper and can lose control in a blur of curse words and flailing arms. Sometimes this happens for no apparent reason, and Lucia then has to be sent to the office to cool down. Ms. Reardon has spoken with Lucia numerous times about this, but nothing changes. After a recent outburst, Lucia and Ms. Reardon decided to try mediation.

During their session, Lucia spoke first and described her concerns about the book report. Ms. Reardon responded that Ivy's book was much longer than Lucia's; that was why it appeared she had to read more than her classmate. Lucia understood that she was mistaken about being treated unfairly.

Ms. Reardon said that she liked Lucia and wanted to help her succeed in school. This made a big impression upon Lucia. Ms. Reardon then brought up Lucia's tantrums. Lucia admitted she had a problem controlling herself sometimes. She said that she got most frustrated when she fell too far behind the rest of the class in her reading. Ms. Reardon suggested some accommodations they could make to prevent this from happening. In addition, teacher and student devised a signal which Lucia could use to let Ms. Reardon know that she was getting frustrated and needed a break. Lucia also agreed to speak with a counselor about her anger.

With encouragement from the mediators (one a teacher, the other an 8th grade student), Lucia expressed her concern that Ms. Reardon only talked about her father and not her mother. Ms. Reardon explained that this was because she had spoken only with Lucia's father. She apologized and agreed to mention both her mother and her father in the future.

At the end of the session, both parties expressed surprise at how easy it had been to mediate. Ms. Reardon shook Lucia's hand with mock seriousness, and the two returned to class with renewed enthusiasm.

Sometimes a teacher and student feel they are working at cross purposes. The teacher wants to help the student learn, but feels like the student resists his or her efforts. The student wants a productive and "hassle-free" education, but experiences the teacher as demanding or unfair. Teachers resolve many of these situations by communicating directly with their students. But each year, most teachers have at least a few students with whom they have particular difficulty communicating. As mediation gains credibility within schools, more teachers look to mediation for assistance with these conflicts.

Though mediating conflicts between students and teachers is usually not the primary focus of school-based mediation efforts, it has been an effective application of the process. Some mediation trainers will not even work with schools unless they educate teachers about mediation and recommend the process to adults as well as students. Refusal to do so indicates to these trainers that:

- Adults in the building do not understand mediation
- Teachers who otherwise might mediate with students will hesitate to do so for fear that administrators and colleagues will perceive them as less competent
- Adults may not support the process even when used for student/student conflicts

Furthermore, it sends a confusing message if students are encouraged to practice supposed "life skills" that their teachers will not apply.

It is essential to note here the unique role that power plays in teacher-student relations, and by extension, in teacher-student mediation. On the one hand, teachers have a considerable degree of social control over their students' lives. With few exceptions, teachers make and enforce classroom rules, determine exactly how students spend their time in school, and dispense rewards and punishments for academic (and social) performance. Despite decades of research showing that teachers who *share* these responsibilities increase students' motivation and performance, many teachers still aspire to be dictators (albeit benevolent ones) within their classrooms.

On the other hand, the assumption that teachers have all the power, and students have none, is inaccurate. There are many sources of power: formal authority, physical force, knowledge, popularity, moral power, charisma, etc. Young people have access to many of these. Every student, for instance, has the power to refuse to learn in class, and it can be as challenging for certain students to give up their hostile attitude towards authority figures as it is for teachers to relinquish their assumed power over students. Participation in mediation does demand that teachers relinquish their apparent power *over*

DON'T LIMIT A CHILD TO YOUR OWN LEARNING, FOR HE WAS BORN IN ANOTHER TIME.

RABBINICAL SAYING

students in order to work *with* them. But the mediation process does not shift the way power is distributed so much as implicitly acknowledge the power that teacher and student each possess.[*]

Even when teachers and administrators begin to embrace mediation, often the most self-assured educators are first to try the process with their students. As individual teachers have success with mediation, their colleagues see that they have little to lose and much to gain by mediating with the students they have been unable to reach. Mediating then becomes a conscious extension of teachers' pedagogy and of a school culture that encourages equal participation and democratic process.[+] In addition to being most effective from an educational standpoint, such a culture increases the likelihood that all of the kinds of challenging cases discussed in this book can be successfully mediated.

For the student and teacher in conflict, simply participating in a mediation session—apart from anything that results from it—can have a tremendous positive impact upon their relationship. Student and teacher relate as equals within the context of the session: people with differing responsibilities, levels of maturity, energy, openness, and wisdom, but as equals nonetheless. This enables them to focus clearly on the issues that create tension between them, and leads to a dramatic change in the quality of their relationship.

Teachers and students often have a new appreciation of one another after participating in mediation. Students appear more deserving of respect; teachers become humanized. As one high school student put it after a session: "It was helpful to hear how a teacher honestly feels, how she reacts inside to what I do. I could see how I would be upset if I were her." The teacher commented: "I understood how there was more going on in his life than I had seen; this was hampering our ability to work together." Regardless of what is agreed upon in the session—even if no resolution is

---

[*] Davis and Salem have noted that by modeling respectful behavior, fostering an open exploration of issues, and recognizing that parties may be dependent upon one another to resolve their conflict, mediators *balance* as well as *acknowledge* power.

[+] One middle school encourages teachers at specific times of the year to provide the mediation coordinator with a list of students with whom they feel they need to mediate.

reached—it is unlikely that student and teacher will ever be depersonalized adversaries again.

Teacher-student mediation also provides a forum for educators to express their professional and personal concern for students. For a variety of reasons, this concern may go unexpressed. In mediation sessions, students often hear their teachers say that they care about them and appreciate their unique strengths. This feels wonderful to students, and it feels just as wonderful to teachers, who may reconnect with their motivation for becoming educators in the first place.

Suggestions for Mediating Conflicts Between Teachers and Students

The following suggestions will help mediators conduct effective teacher-student sessions:

Preliminary Actions

- **Educate the staff.** The importance of educating all teachers about mediation, before any individual teacher utilizes the process, cannot be underestimated. Teachers will mediate only if they are informed about and comfortable with it. One concern expressed about mediating between teachers and students—that teachers will form a negative opinion of (and treat unfairly) any student who asks to mediate with them—is much less likely when teachers are educated about the process.

Intake

- **Be wary of mediating disputes that involve a teacher allegedly harassing a student.** Students often experience their teachers as harassing them, and many of these conflicts are appropriate for mediation. Be sure to do a careful intake before scheduling any teacher-student mediation, however. If it appears that a teacher is intentionally and maliciously harassing a student, encourage the student to report their concerns to counselors and school administrators first. After an investigation and subsequent actions, if all parties (as well as the mediation coordinator, mediators, administrators, and the student's guardians) feel it is appropriate, the mediation process can be used.

- **Keep the mediation process voluntary.** Though some schools *require* that students in conflict *attend* a mediation session, it is essential that teachers feel that their participation is completely voluntary. Most educators are already nervous about trying mediation with their students. Forcing them to mediate would be counterproductive. Concerns about being coerced to mediate may also lead teachers to resist efforts to implement a peer mediation program for students.

- **Minimize the use of the term "mediation" when appropriate.** Some teachers do not hesitate to ask counselors to facilitate meetings between themselves and students with whom they are having difficulty. Even though the counselors serve as mediators in this context, these same teachers might refuse to participate if they were aware that they were "mediating" with their students. Counselor/mediators report that as long as expectations are clear, teachers are more likely to participate if they call the work a "meeting" rather than a "mediation session."

Mediator Selection

- **Select mediators carefully.** In student-teacher mediation, having an adult and a student co-mediate and "mirror" the parties is usually preferable. Using solely student or adult mediators tends to make the non-represented party uncomfortable and hesitant to invest in the process. Some additional ideas:

  —It can be awkward for student mediators to work with teacher parties. Student mediators must present themselves confidently and not be too deferential. "Ms. Chung and I are experienced mediators and we look forward to serving you today" is better than "Thank you for letting me [a lowly student like myself] serve you."

  —A special caution for teacher mediators: Only if they have the appropriate relationship with the teacher party (a relationship characterized either by great trust or by little contact) will they be able to remain unbiased without angering their colleague.

Although not preferable, using only adult mediators has been effective when teachers will not accept student mediators.

During the Session

- **Support parties' efforts.** Mediators always encourage parties, but this is even more essential when students and teachers mediate. Students need courage to negotiate with teachers who are typically much older. Take extra care to make them feel comfortable. As the ostensibly more powerful party, teachers also take risks by participating in the process. In addition to mediators' support and encouragement, teachers need acknowledgment that though they may be equals in the context of mediation, they have unique levels of responsibility and experience within the school.

- **Practice "cross-communication."** When "cross-communicating," the adult mediator addresses and summarizes the student party's concerns while the student mediator does the same for the adult party. This practice builds parties' trust in the mediators and ultimately in each other.

- **Prepare for an imbalance in communication skills.** Teachers are generally more confident and communicative than students, especially younger students. Mediators manage this imbalance in a number of ways. Some encourage students to speak first in the joint session to ensure that their initial mediation experience is not sitting and listening to their teacher complain about them. Others, expecting student parties to feel intimidated initially, ask teachers to give an overview of the situation before inviting students to speak. Private sessions are also a helpful and sometimes essential tool. Be sure to hold sessions in a neutral setting and sit parties as equals around the table.

- **Keep the discussion as specific as possible.** One challenging aspect of student-teacher mediation is that parties tend to make broad generaliza-

> MANY PROMISING RECONCILIATIONS HAVE BROKEN DOWN BECAUSE WHILE BOTH PARTIES CAME PREPARED TO FORGIVE, NEITHER PARTY CAME PREPARED TO BE FORGIVEN.
>
> CHARLES WILLIAMS

tions about one another. Students assert that they have a "bad teacher"; teachers say they are working with an "unmotivated student." This can have disastrous consequences if allowed to persist. Help parties focus by asking: "What specifically does he do as a teacher that you don't like?" or "Describe a specific time that you felt Polly behaved inappropriately."

- **Remain aware of both your own and the parties' biases.** This can be one of the biggest challenges in these cases. It is common in student-teacher mediation for student mediators to identify with the student and adults mediators to identify with the teacher. Student mediators might also identify with a teacher's perspective because they have been socialized to accept teacher control of students. Guard against this.

There is no guarantee that teachers and students will be able to resolve their conflicts through mediation. But when student/teacher teams co-mediate these cases, the process has a clarity of form and function—and a level of effectiveness—which can exceed the more traditional method of resolving teacher-student conflicts: conferences with administrators or counselors. Once understood, the potential benefits of mediation make it attractive to teachers and students alike.

Resources

Video

Peer Mediation in Action
Colorado School Mediation Project
3970 Broadway, Suite B3
Boulder, CO 80304
(303) 444-7671
web site: www.csmp.org
This video contains one of the only student-teacher mediation simulations available.

Checklist
MEDIATING CONFLICTS BETWEEN STUDENTS AND TEACHERS

INTAKE

✓ Be wary of mediating disputes that involve a teacher allegedly harassing a student (125)

✓ Ensure that teachers feel that their participation in mediation is completely voluntary (126)

✓ Minimize the use of the term "mediation" when appropriate (126)

MEDIATOR SELECTION

✓ Assign an adult and a student to co-mediate and "mirror" the parties when possible (126)

✓ Select student mediators who are comfortable working with adults (126)

✓ Use only adult mediators when teacher parties will not accept student mediators (127)

✓ For teacher mediators: Only if you have a relationship with the teacher party characterized either by great trust or by little contact will you be able to remain unbiased without angering your teaching colleague (126)

DURING THE SESSION

✓ Take extra care to make parties feel comfortable and support their efforts (127)

✓ Student mediators should present themselves confidently and do not be overly deferential to teachers (126)

✓ Prepare to manage an imbalance in communication skills: (127)

✓ Encourage student parties to speak first (127)

✓ If student parties seem intimidated at the start, ask teacher parties to give an overview of the situation before student parties speak (127)

✓ Practice "cross-communication" initially: The adult mediator addresses and summarizes the student party's concerns while the student mediator does the same for the teacher party (127)

✓ Keep the discussion as specific as possible, asking, "What specifically does he do that you don't like?" (127)

✓ Remain aware of both your own and the parties' biases (128)

7

MEDIATING
CONFLICTS
BETWEEN
STUDENTS AND
THEIR PARENTS

WRITTEN WITH MELISSA BRODRICK

*Odallys Santiago used to think she had an extraordinary rela-
tionship with her 16 year old son, Wilfredo. They often talked
and laughed together, and she had the sense that they <u>liked</u> as
well as loved each other. But now she doesn't even recognize him.
He comes home at 3 a.m. on Friday and Saturday nights despite
his 12 p.m. curfew. Odallys found some "papers" in his room that
are used for drugs. And his increasing moodiness and disrespect
means that they can hardly do what they always did so well:
<u>communicate</u>. Odallys was beginning to feel like she could not
handle Wilfredo anymore.*

*The last straw came during an argument about school. Mr.
Sinese, Wilfredo's guidance counselor, had informed her that
Wilfredo was flunking a number of courses. He said that
Wilfredo often came to school late, missing the classes entirely.
Odallys tried to talk with Wilfredo about this, but he avoided
both her and the subject. When she insisted that they discuss it
over dinner, Wilfredo got so upset that he threw his plate
against the wall and stormed out of the house. Right then,
Odallys knew there was no turning back. Things had to change,
and she needed help.*

Conflicts are a frequent occurrence between teenaged students and their parents. As a time of great change for young people and those who love them, adolescence leaves parent and child with differing expectations of each other's roles and responsibilities. The concrete issues that precipitate these conflicts usually involve topics like curfew, chores, friends, boyfriends/girlfriends, communication, school performance and attendance, and money/employment. But while every conflict between a parent and teen is unique, common underlying concerns about love, respect, authority, independence, trust, responsibility, and safety characterize most of them. For some families, conflicts are complicated by difficult family issues such as divorce or remarriage, poverty and lack of economic opportunity, or family relocation.

NO PEOPLE ARE EVER
AS DIVIDED AS THOSE
OF THE SAME BLOOD.
MAVIS GALLANT

In 1980, the first parent-child mediation program was established to help families negotiate this difficult terrain.* Many similar efforts followed. These programs were initially designed to provide an alternative to families who had become involved with the juvenile courts because of behaviors known as status offenses: truancy from school, running away from home, and chronic "acting out." Most programs were affiliated with a human service agency and worked very closely with their local court.

As the parent-child mediation concept spread across the country, however, strategies were developed to help families resolve conflicts *before* they become involved with the judicial system. These efforts were motivated by the belief that families had not only the right, but with minimal assistance, the ability to create their own solutions to the problems they faced. A 1985 study bore this out: 85% of the parents and children participating in mediation reached agreements, and 75% of those agreements were effectively implemented by family members.[28]

---

* The pioneering program was the Children's Hearings Project based in Cambridge, Massachusetts. Unfortunately, the program is no longer in existence.

Why Offer Student-Parent Mediation at School?

Parent-child (or more accurately, parent-teen) mediation programs share school-based mediation's roots in the community mediation movement. As a result, the programs share a similar design: Coordinators conduct intake interviews, supervise sessions, and follow up on cases, and a diverse pool of volunteer co-mediators is used to mediate. Even the parent-teen mediation process is virtually identical to the one utilized by school mediators.

Schools have generally been reluctant to become involved in family conflicts, understanding their mission to be the education of children, not families. But as the effects of a long list of social problems spill into the classroom, increasing numbers of educators understand that supporting a student's family and community furthers the goal of educating the student. Though still uncommon, student-parent mediation services, offered at school, can be one such method of support.

For many reasons, schools are uniquely suited to provide mediation services to parents and their adolescent children. Consider:

—**School is one of the central issues over which parents and teenagers disagree.** Grades, attendance, behavior, homework, attitude, tardiness: These education-related issues are all high on the list of subjects that create conflict at home.

—**School personnel may have already won students' trust.** Young people spend more time at school than any other place except their homes. With so much time to interact with students (and to observe them interacting with peers and adults) perceptive educators come to know their charges quite well. Some teachers, held in high esteem and trusted by students, hear all about their students' difficulties at home. These educators can serve as a bridge between parent and teen and either assist them directly or help them identify additional resources.

—**Schools have a natural alliance with parents.** Educators and parents have the same fundamental goal for students: the best education possible. As such, teachers' and parents' concerns often overlap. Both want to see students come to school on time, do their homework, behave appropriately and so on. Because parents already look to schools for support with education related issues, they may be more likely to utilize school-based services than if they are referred to a separate agency.

—**School issues provide a "hook" to get families into mediation.** Barring a crisis, concerns about privacy and trust, lack of information and resources, and simple habit all combine to prevent most families from seeking outside assistance for their internal conflicts. Behavior problems or academic difficulties at school provide a focus that can get parents and children in the mediator's office. Once there, they may avail themselves of the opportunity to discuss other, chronic difficulties, often for the first time.

—**Schools with effective peer mediation programs already have most of the resources needed to conduct student-parent mediation sessions.** Not only do these schools have coordinators, mediators, offices, etc., but students and parents may be familiar with mediation from the peer mediation program's outreach efforts. Advanced training for mediators and some logistical modifications are often the only additions necessary to enable school-based mediators to conduct parent-teen mediation sessions.

—**Schools have easy access to the people students respect most: their peers!** Peer pressure is tremendous during adolescence. Teenagers look to their peers to determine not only what to wear, but what to think and how to behave. School mediation programs use this to their advantage and turn what is commonly a negative influence into a positive force. The same can be accomplished by including a student co-mediator in parent-teen sessions. With additional training in adolescent issues and family dynamics, student mediators are often able to build trust with teenage parties more readily than adult mediators. And having a student and an adult co-mediate demonstrates for families that "young and old" can get along.

The Challenges of Mediating Student-Parent Conflicts at School

Despite these advantages, there are considerable challenges to mediating parent-teen disputes in schools. The obstacles that these cases present include:

- **Psychological depth.** Psychological need motivates parties in all conflicts, but few relationships are as psychologically complex as that between parent and child. Parent-teen conflicts have as much to do with who parties are as what they have done, and behaviors and beliefs that contribute to them have roots deep in parties' characters. Battles over homework, for instance, might be attributable to a parent's unhealthy need for control; a student's inappropriate behavior might be motivated by self-destructive urges. Parties may not be psychologically ready or willing to acknowledge these factors, nor is mediation the proper forum for exploring them.

  Experienced parent-teen mediators know that mediation, helpful as it may be, often just scratches the surface of what families need. These disputes are more difficult to resolve than the average student dispute, and families may need on-going services (counseling, housing assistance) that school-based mediation programs are not able to provide.

- **Many inter-related issues.** The issues in typical parent-teen disputes—school, chores, work, friends, romance, money—are wide ranging and interconnected. This can pose a challenge for school-based mediators. For though parents and children may be willing to discuss school-related issues in the school setting, they may be unwilling to discuss the associated private issues that trouble them. Progress on the school issues may be dependent upon reaching some understanding about the others. (A student, for example, may be unwilling to discuss his friends in mediation, friends that the parent may feel have a negative influence on the student's academic performance.) Mediators can find it challenging to get permission to guide parties where they appear to need to go.

- **Subtle power dynamics.** Power is a key theme in parent-teen relations. The common assumption that parents have more of it than their children may be incorrect, however. A young person who does not go to school, who frequently runs away, or who uses violent language at home exercises considerable power in the relationship. In fact, parents often come to mediation because they feel they have lost the ability to control their children. It takes a discerning mediator to understand this dynamic and manage it appropriately.

- **Logistics.** The way most schools are structured presents considerable obstacles to mediating student-parent disputes. For one, schools are open only on weekdays while most parents, because of work commitments, prefer to mediate in the evenings or on weekends. In addition, school-based coordinators and mediators usually work against the clock: The longer they mediate, the more they neglect their other responsibilities. Parent-teen mediation, involving extensive preparatory work, two to four hour meetings, and disputes that may require multiple sessions, can demand too much of these volunteers' time.

EVERYONE LIKES TO
THINK HE HAS DONE
REASONABLY WELL IN
LIFE, SO THAT IT
COMES AS A SHOCK
TO FIND OUR CHIL-
DREN BELIEVING DIF-
FERENTLY. THE TEMP-
TATION IS TO TUNE
THEM OUT; IT TAKES
MUCH MORE COURAGE
TO LISTEN.

JOHN D. ROCKEFELLER

Creating Community-School Partnerships

Before attempting to meet these challenges, school mediators should consider whether, on balance, mediation services could be better provided to families by a parent-teen mediation program in the community. These programs have some clear strengths, including that:

—The affiliated mediators have training that is specifically geared towards parent-teen mediation.

—The community program's case coordinator will have ample time to devote to this work and may be better able to help families access additional services.

—Mediation sessions can be conducted in the evenings to accommodate working family members.

—Sessions can be conducted at a local site that is as accessible to families as the school building.

—If they do not do so already, the community program may be willing to train the school's peer mediators to co-mediate disputes with an adult.

When possible, enter into a collaborative relationship with a local parent-teen program. They will certainly appreciate working with an excellent referral source such as the school, a referral source that has both the knowledge and often the faith and trust of families. Working together might also prove to be an effective strategy to raise the funds necessary to maintain both the parent-teen and the school-based mediation efforts.

School/community mediation partnerships have created unique approaches to identifying families that might benefit from parent-teen mediation. One such partnership set up a Truancy Review Board to review truancy records on a bi-monthly basis, identify at-risk students early, and provide them with the support they needed. Included on the board were truant and probation officers, a variety of school personnel, and a representative from the community-based parent-teen mediation program. By involving the parent-teen mediation program so early, the opportunity for mediation to be truly preventive was greatly increased.

Suggestions for Mediating Conflicts Between Students and their Parents

Sabeena has not been getting along with her dad, John. The main problem is that she hates his new girlfriend, Roxanne. Roxanne is always in a foul mood, she is always at their house, and it is impossible to be with her dad alone. Sabeena goes home as little as possible because of this, sleeping over at her girlfriend Lisa's house most nights. Once Sabeena stayed with her boyfriend, Minh, but it was a hassle because he wanted to have sex. Sabeena, who is afraid of getting pregnant, had to keep putting him off and it was just not worth going over there.

Ever since Sabeena's mother died, John is nervous about things. He criticizes Sabeena all the time about school and work and coming home. He is also prejudiced, and he constantly tries to get her to break up with Minh because Minh is Asian and Sabeena is black. This is another reason she does not go home much.

Last week Sabeena was caught hanging out in the park during school hours. She actually likes 8th grade, and her grades are better than ever. But sometimes she just needs to take a break and "collect her thoughts" (as Ms. Binoche, her English teacher, says). She has gone to the park only a few times.

The assistant principal was really upset, however, and so was Sabeena's dad when he found out. He threatened to pull her out of the middle school and send her to the local Catholic school. The assistant principal told Sabeena he was going to have to punish her, but he also told her about mediation. It sounded like an okay thing to her, especially since one of the mediators was a kid. Her dad was willing to try the mediation as well. Perhaps that would help.

Many communities do not have a parent-teen mediation program that is easily accessible. If schools in these communities want to encourage families to mediate, they must meet the challenges associated with parent-teen mediation and offer the services themselves. By capitalizing on a school program's strengths, mediators can overcome the obstacles and offer very effective services. Here are some suggestions:

Logistics

Though some parents are able to mediate during the school day, to make their service accessible, school-based mediators need to be available during non-school hours. Making this happen is usually more a question of commitment than logistics. Most school mediators, whether student or adult, are volunteers and so contractual issues with school employees are not a concern. Because school buildings are often empty in the evening but for custodial staff, this is usually not a problem either. With the necessary administrative support, it should be possible to overcome the hurdles associated with logistics.

Intake

Skilled intake interviewing is essential in all of the more challenging cases that school mediators face, and parent-teen cases are no exception. Key to an effective intake process is the coordinator. Parent-teen case coordinators must have the skill and sensitivity to establish the safe environment that is critical to mediation's success. They must have ample time to meet with all family members, explain the process, and determine whether mediation is appropriate. Parent-teen coordinators may also help families access additional services before and after mediation.

In addition to the standard school-based approach to intake interviewing, coordinators must be sure to:

- **Identify additional parties.** It is critical that all stakeholders participate in mediation sessions. In parent-teen mediation, who the stakeholders are is not always clear. Must both parents attend? How about siblings with a stake in the outcome of the mediation? Or live-in partners, stepparents or grandparents who help raise the student? If the student divides his or her time between two households, should both parents be encouraged to attend? When the issues warrant it, even friends of the teen (including a boyfriend or girlfriend) or a school support person might be invited for one of the sessions. Working together with the parties one has identified, consider the scope (school, home, both) and severity of the issues to be discussed. Without key individuals present, there is a risk that parties might create agreements that are limited by incomplete information or which may later be undermined by absent parties.

Students and Parents

- **Explore parties' willingness to discuss non-school related issues.**
  Open-ended questions like "Overall, how is your relationship with your
  daughter?" may uncover concerns unrelated to the educational issues that
  bring parties to the interview. Even when parties do not mention other
  issues, explain that family conflicts are complex and often involve a set of
  interconnected concerns. Reconciliation is more likely when parties discuss relevant concerns openly and honestly. Do not push too hard during
  intake, however. Once parties are in the session, they might feel comfortable raising issues that were not mentioned during this early phase.

- **Inform parties that mediation is not counseling.** Mediation is a short
  term, *interpersonal* process that helps "parties" understand one another
  and if they so desire, create concrete resolutions to their shared problems.
  Counseling is a relatively long-term, *intrapersonal* process that helps
  "clients" understand themselves and improve their ability to meet their
  own needs. It is essential to explain this difference to parties. Some will
  be relieved to hear this and will be more likely to try mediation. Others
  may need this information so that they do not attempt to turn the mediators into family therapists. Mediation can, however, be a first step that
  helps families decide to pursue counseling.

- **Inform parties about confidentiality.** It is especially important to ensure
  that students and their parents understand the limits of confidentiality in
  mediation. Many parent-teen mediation programs require parties to sign
  a so called "agreement-to-participate" form which outlines essential information about confidentiality and other aspects of the mediation process.
  School-based mediators should do the same when handling family disputes. Most school-based programs do not protect information that is
  life-threatening or illegal. Mediators who are educators may also be
  "mandated reporters" (mandated by law to inform authorities if they have
  suspicions concerning child abuse or neglect).

- **Provide referrals for additional support.** Prepare a comprehensive list of
  local resources in advance and look for opportunities to link family mem-

bers with other beneficial services. The resources may be school-based (such as academic tutors or school counselors) or community-based (human service agencies, parenting classes, or after-school programs).

Toward the conclusion of the intake interview, both with the parties and in private, consider whether mediation is appropriate. Aside from concerns specific to each case, the general and commonsense limits to parent-teen mediation include when:

1. A key family member is unwilling or unavailable to participate in the sessions.
2. A family member, because of age, confidence, or ability, is unable to advocate effectively for him or herself (most family mediators will not work with children under 12 years of age as a primary party).
3. Issues such as alcohol or drug addiction, physical/sexual abuse, or mental illness indicate that law enforcement or social service agencies would be more appropriate.

It is essential to devise an effective follow-up program *prior to* mediating a single student-parent conflict. Plan on monitoring agreements by contacting family members soon after they conclude the mediation. Some programs call parties numerous times over a period of six months. If family members continue to have problems, invite them back to mediate and/or refer them to additional services.

Mediator Selection

- **Use only mature mediators.** As usual, coordinators strive to assign mediators that "mirror" the parties. For parent-teen disputes, that would mean using a young person and an adult to co-mediate. The emotional complexity of these conflicts, however, combined with adults' potential reticence to discuss "family business" with another young person, leads some coordinators to hesitate to assign students to these cases. High school students can effectively mediate parent-teen disputes. But only excep-

WHEN I WAS A BOY OF FOURTEEN, MY FATHER WAS SO IGNORANT I COULD HARDLY STAND TO HAVE THE OLD MAN AROUND. BUT WHEN I GOT TO BE TWENTY-ONE, I WAS ASTONISHED AT HOW MUCH THE OLD MAN HAD LEARNED IN SEVEN YEARS.

MARK TWAIN

tional student mediators are prepared to elicit personal information from a parent, to remain unbiased after listening to disturbing family histories, and to handle unexpected issues such as alcoholism or abuse should they arise. If such student mediators are not available, use exclusively experienced adults to mediate.

- **Provide additional training.** While the best school-based mediators may be able to mediate parent-teen disputes without additional training, all mediators would benefit greatly from it. Many parent-teen programs require that beginning mediators apprentice with more experienced colleagues to receive guidance and supervision. Some training should be informational and focus on topics such as:
  —Typical adolescent issues and family dynamics
  —The role of the coordinator in working with families
  —Substance abuse, physical abuse, and sexual abuse: how they present themselves in mediation, and how to handle it when they do.
  —Information about cultural diversity (if not already covered in basic training)
  —An overview of the local court and social service systems

The bulk of the advanced training should concentrate on the *process* of mediating family conflicts. Use roleplays, small group-problem solving, and discussions to help mediators explore the process modifications suggested below.

During the Session

- **Create a comfortable environment.** The generation gap and accompanying power dynamics between students and their parents demand that mediators give special attention to establishing a positive feeling in the room. Set a tone of inclusiveness by asking parties how they would like to be addressed (don't take for granted that one can use adults' first names), using language that is comfortable for everyone, and being sensitive to cultural factors. The best mediators manage to defer to adults and empower young people at the same time.

- **Highlight deeper themes.** At the start of family mediation, parties often begin by complaining about the concrete behaviors that have brought them to mediation: "My mother is always yelling at me," or "She refuses to get up to go to school, no matter how often I pester her." Although these behaviors are important, help parties articulate the underlying concerns raised by these behaviors (respect, independence, trust, responsibility, etc.). These larger issues provide a context that enables parties to understand one another, thereby increasing the likelihood that they will be able to work together to resolve their difficulties.

- **Strengthen parties' ability to communicate directly.** Learning to communicate is important for all parties who have an ongoing relationship. For parents and children, who usually live under the same roof and are emotionally linked in the most profound of ways, it is essential. Be sure to help parties consider how to communicate effectively during the session and beyond. It is common for parent-teen agreements to include communication ground rules as well as scheduled "family time" and ways to deal with future conflicts (time-outs, family meetings, etc.). Considering that the continual changes of adolescence mean that what is acceptable to parties now may be unacceptable in six months, building families' capacity to solve their own problems is all the more important.

- **Encourage discussion of non-school related issues.** As discussed above, school-based mediators should be prepared to help students and their parents discuss the range of their concerns: curfew, chores, money, friends, work, sexuality, and so on. At the start of the session, explain that unexpected issues may arise and that mediation might be a very helpful forum in which to discuss them. If mediators create a comfortable environment, many families will appreciate the opportunity to have an unbiased facilitator help them confront these difficulties. If parties prefer not to address these issues, defer to their wishes.

- **Utilize private sessions skillfully.** The power dynamics, increased number of parties, and highly charged atmosphere of parent-teen conflicts lead many mediators to utilize private sessions quite extensively. Private sessions provide parties with space to vent their emotions, reveal new information and calmly consider their situation. Young people especially might feel more comfortable discussing sensitive issues in private rather than in front of their parents. When two parents are involved, some mediators conduct a separate private session with each parent to determine whether they are in agreement. Do not rely too heavily on private sessions, however. Important steps towards understanding and improved communication take place during joint sessions. Watch parties closely and be sure to create opportunities for direct discussions between parent/s and child/ren. Co-mediators can model collaboration and facilitate healthy discussion between family members.

- **Help parties maintain their focus.** Parent-child conflicts stir deep emotions. When parties express their feelings, it can free them to think more clearly and learn about the impact of their behavior. But parent-teen mediators must ensure that the process does not become a counseling session. The basic question to ask is this: Will parties' statements help family members understand one another and resolve their dispute? If they will not, then gently guide them back to the dispute. Parties who identify a need to talk more about their feelings can be encouraged to seek a counselor's assistance. (The program coordinator should be able to assist families in accessing such services.) Advanced training, experience and instinct all help mediators gauge when to limit time spent exploring parties' emotions.

- **Prevent parties from making decisions when they are over-tired.** Unlike mediations between students, which often conclude in less than an hour, parent-teen mediation sessions may last two to four hours and require as many as four separate sessions. The scope of issues, the complexity of the relationships and the fact that there may be many family members present all contribute to the longer nature of these mediations. Parent-teen mediators must be aware of the risk of fatigue for all involved and provide breaks whenever necessary. In addition, consider creating provisional agreements that family members can try and then return to mediation.

The mediation sessions were more difficult than either Sabeena or her dad, John, had expected. The mediators were nice, though. They had met with them twice so far. One mediator was a student from the high school, and the other was a science teacher that Sabeena didn't know, Mr. Giotti.

The first session took almost three hours. First the mediators talked about what mediation was and asked how they wanted it to work. Then Sabeena talked and said how she knew that being at the park was wrong, but she didn't think that it was a big deal. She was still getting good grades and everything. When it was John's turn, he mostly spoke about how mad he was. Sabeena tried to defend herself, but her dad yelled at her. Then Sabeena started to cry. Then her dad got really quiet. The mediators tried to help them talk, but Sabeena didn't want to talk anymore.

Eventually the mediators met with each of them privately. Sabeena hesitated to speak in her meeting, but pretty soon she was telling the mediators everything: about Minh, about Roxanne, about her mother dying, everything. The mediators listened really well, and they helped her realize that she felt like her Dad didn't care about her. All he did was criticize. The mediators encouraged Sabeena to tell her dad as much of this as she could.

In John's private meeting, he mostly talked about how concerned he was about Sabeena. John felt she was neglecting her studies and testing all the rules in the house and at school. Most importantly, John said he felt Sabeena was cutting herself off from the family. He explained that she had a boyfriend that he didn't approve of, and Sabeena often didn't come home at night. Although the mother of one of Sabeena's girlfriends usually called to inform him that Sabeena was there, he feared that she was sleeping at this boy's house some nights. He felt like he could not trust her.

When Sabeena and her dad met together again with the mediators, the conversation started rough but then got smoother. They began by arguing about Minh, but the mediators cut in and helped them talk one at a time. John was relieved to find out that Sabeena wasn't sleeping at Minh's house (Sabeena didn't mention the one time that she had). In the end John agreed to at least meet Minh. Sabeena agreed to not leave school anymore and keep her grades up. She said she wanted her dad to be able to trust her again.

Sabeena then said it bothered her how much John criticized her. He said, "What else am I supposed to do when you behave the way you have been? If you started behaving responsibly, I would try to criticize you less!" John wanted to speak about Sabeena sleeping at home more, but it was time to end. The mediators wrote some things down about what had been said and scheduled another meeting for the next week.

John and Sabeena spent most of the time together, not in separate meetings, during the second mediation. At one point both Sabeena and her dad started to cry about her mother dying and how much they missed her. This was good because they didn't really talk about Sabeena's mother that much anymore. The mediators asked if they wanted to speak more about their feelings with a counselor. Sabeena said yes, she would. John said no.

The rest of the meeting they mostly spoke about Roxanne. Sabeena said she didn't like her. John said that although Sabeena was much more important to him than Roxanne, he was not willing to stop seeing Roxanne. John was delighted that Sabeena had slept at home a couple of nights the previous week, and Sabeena said that her dad wasn't criticizing her as much. When time ran out they decided to schedule one more session and invite Roxanne to come too.

John hasn't called to schedule the third session yet, but from Sabeena's perspective, things are better at home already. Roxanne is not around every night. A half dozen times Sabeena has come home, spent time with her dad watching TV or something, and slept in her own room. Her dad wasn't very nice when he met Minh, and John still criticizes her sometimes, but things are definitely better. The counselor is helping Sabeena feel better about her life and understand her dad a little more. Sabeena hopes her dad schedules the next mediation session.

Schools have a unique position relative to students and their families. Pioneering school mediators take advantage of this when they begin to conduct parent-teen mediation sessions at school. The obstacles, though real, are not so great that they cannot be overcome. Parent-teen mediation efforts can keep troubled families together longer, help students resolve the home-based concerns that distract them from their studies, and enable schools to become a more vital part of the communities they serve.

Resources

Organizations

National Association for Community Mediation (NAFCM)
1527 New Hampshire Ave, NW
Washington, DC 20036
(202) 667-9700
email: nafcm@nafcm.org
Provides information about local community mediation programs as well as other relevant local associations

Academy of Family Mediators
5 Militia Drive
Lexington, MA 02421
(781) 674-2663
web site: www.mediators.org

I KNOW WHY FAMILIES WERE CREATED, WITH ALL THEIR IMPERFECTIONS. THEY HUMANIZE YOU. THEY ARE MADE TO MAKE YOU FORGET YOURSELF OCCASIONALLY, SO THAT THE BEAUTIFUL BALANCE OF LIFE IS NOT DESTROYED.

ANAIS NIN

Checklist
MEDIATING CONFLICTS BETWEEN STUDENTS AND THEIR PARENTS

INTAKE

✓ Prepare a comprehensive list of local resources in advance (140)

✓ Look for opportunities to link family members with other beneficial services (140)

✓ Identify and contact additional parties (139)

✓ Make ample time to meet with all family members and help them determine whether mediation is appropriate (139)

✓ Explore parties' willingness to discuss non-school related issues, asking open-ended questions such as, "Overall, how is your relationship with your daughter?" (140)

✓ Ensure that parties understand that mediation is not counseling (140)

✓ Inform parties about the confidentiality policy and its limitations (140)

✓ Prior to mediating a single student-parent conflict, devise an effective follow-up program that includes a system for monitoring agreements (141)

Parent-teen mediation is not advisable when: (141)

1. A key family member is unwilling or unavailable to participate in the sessions

2. A family member, because of age, confidence, or ability, is unable to advocate effectively for him or herself

3. Issues such as alcohol or drug addiction, physical/sexual abuse, or mental illness indicate that law enforcement or social service agencies would be more appropriate than school-based mediation

MEDIATOR SELECTION

✓ Provide additional training on: (142)
- Typical adolescent issues and family dynamics
- The role of the coordinator in working with families
- Substance abuse, physical abuse, and sexual abuse
- The local court and social service systems

✓ Use primarily adults to mediate because of parent-teen disputes' emotional complexity and many adult parties' reticence to discuss "family business" with young people (141)

✓ Exceptional student mediators can mediate parent-teen conflicts, so long as they can: (141)
  • Elicit personal information from a parent
  • Remain unbiased after listening to disturbing family histories
  • Handle strong emotions and unexpected issues such as alcoholism or abuse

DURING THE SESSION

✓ Create a comfortable environment (142)

✓ Help parties articulate underlying concerns and deeper themes (143)

✓ Strengthen parties' ability to communicate directly by encouraging them to do so during the session (143)

✓ Encourage discussion of non-school related issues (143)

✓ Utilize private sessions skillfully (143)

✓ Help parties maintain their focus (144)

✓ Prevent parties from making decisions when they are over-tired (144)

Students and Parents

MEDIATING CONFLICTS INVOLVING LARGE GROUPS

With the rapid expansion of school-based mediation programs across North America, many secondary schools now train students and staff to mediate disputes between two individuals. But it is not unusual for disputes to occur that involve a dozen and occasionally even one hundred parties. These large group disputes often involve prejudice in some form, but they erupt over the range of human concerns. Mediating between *groups* rather than between individuals provides a unique challenge to school-based mediators and mediation programs.

One point must be stressed at the outset: Most large group disputes among students arise either from festering interpersonal conflicts or from structural inequities within a school. In fact, the incidence of large group conflicts usually indicates that there are systemic problems in the way a school and its community address the concerns of young people. Large group conflicts are a symptom; the underlying disease may be attributable to many factors. Consider:

    —Do students find school engaging and relevant?

    —Are there adults in the school whom students trust?

    —Does the school reach out to students pro-actively to help them
       resolve conflicts before they escalate?

    —Is the faculty representative of the diversity found in the student body?

    —Do students and adults feel safe and appreciated in school?

—Do parents and the wider community make education a priority? Merely mediating a particular dispute will not prevent large group disputes from occurring in a school. A more comprehensive intervention is usually necessary.

When there are approximately three to eight parties in conflict—what can be called "small group" disputes—coordinators and mediators usually employ the same process used for disputes that involve two parties: Each party gets an opportunity to speak and be heard (even if four people are on one "side" of dispute, each person is encouraged to tell his or her version of events), and the same basic steps of the process are followed.

Recommended adjustments for small group disputes include:
- Allow more time for preparation.
- Increase the involvement of adults as mediators or as coordinators present during sessions.
- If students are used to mediate, select the school's most skilled student mediators.
- Schedule more time for the session.
- Increase the use of private sessions, including preliminary private sessions with individuals or groups prior to a joint session.
- Encourage parties to participate in the process as individuals, not only as a member of a group. Rather than collaboratively explain the group's perspective, each party receives ample opportunity to explain his or her personal perspective on the conflict.
- Use extra caution to prevent the victimization of parties who are out-numbered. If the conflict involves one party vs. four parties, this may mean having the one party mediate separately with each of the four parties.
- Increase the attention and support given to parties after the session.

As the number of parties increase, however, so does the complexity of the process. Consider the difference between transporting two groups of people from one side of town to the other. For a group consisting of only two people, one would use a car. The size of the second group, forty individuals, would necessitate using a bus. There are significant ways in which bus travel differs from passenger car travel: coordinating the arrival and departure of 40 bus passengers takes a great deal *more planning* than two car passengers; travel on a bus requires *increased supervision* and possibly *unique rules of behavior*; and bus drivers must have *additional skills and training* beyond that required for a passenger car license.

Large group disputes are to two-party disputes what bus travel is to car travel. Just a few of the ways in which large group disputes are more complicated include:

1. The basic logistics—getting all of the parties in the same room at the same time—can be very challenging.
2. There are more perspectives to hear and understand.
3. There are potentially more issues.
4. The issues involved may be more complex.
5. There can be numerous, discrete interpersonal conflicts contained within a large group dispute.
6. Parties within a group may disagree *with one another* as well as with people from other groups.
7. There is a greater potential for interpersonal violence because people in groups (especially *young* people in groups) may behave in ways they wouldn't individually.
8. It is harder to maintain control. When parties argue in interpersonal disputes, it is relatively easy to get them to stop. But when 12 people are yelling, spread throughout a group of 45, it is much more difficult to control.
9. Large group disputes take more time both per session and in the number of sessions. This can take a toll on mediators and parties.

Coordinators and mediators manage these challenges by modifying the basic process used for disputes involving only two parties. This chapter presents those strategic modifications in rough chronological order.

Large Groups

WORDS ARE A FORM OF ACTION CAPABLE OF INFLUENCING CHANGE.

INGRID BENGIS

Let's first look at a typical large group conflict, presented from the perspective of one of the parties. We will refer back to this example as we explore the strategies used to mediate large group conflicts.

> *My name is Christine Jones. I am a high school sophomore, and I have lived in Yorkville my entire life.* * *I am not the best student at Yorkville High School, but my life has been fairly typical and, I would say, fairly happy. Things began to get difficult last year when I started dating a guy named Billie Fernandez. Billie, a junior, is Cape Verdean, which means he is partly black. I am white. This has caused the problems.*
>
> *The biggest problem has been with my brother, Nate. Nate is kind of a tough kid who thinks he is great. He is also prejudiced. He and his friends have bothered me about Billie from the start. They tease me and tell me not to date Billie, and Nate even locked me out of our house once, saying I should not come home until I started acting white and "got the dark scum off of my skin." It hasn't helped that my mother, Ruth, and my stepfather, Raymond, don't like black people either and make negative comments.*
>
> *Over the last six months things have gotten worse. Nate's friends have been picking on Billie and his friends, so now whole <u>groups</u> of kids are involved. Nate is on the wrestling team and he is friendly with the athletic kids at school. Billie, on the other hand, has never played sports; his friends are kind of all mixed and most of them are not very physically fit. Not all of them are kids of color either; a fair number of them are white. Still, Nate and his buddies—especially this skinhead guy Frank—call Billie and his friends 'black.' That is how stupid they are.*

---

* A small city located twenty miles from a major industrial center, the fictional city of Yorkville is, like many small cities, a community in transition. Factories that were the biggest employers in town have long since closed. Most people commute to work and do not know their neighbors, and the religious, ethnic and racial diversity of the city has increased dramatically over the last fifteen years.

Large Groups

The problem has even gone beyond the "black/white" issue. Nate and his friends are mostly "jocks," and Billie and his group of friends (including me) are part of the "alternative" crowd. Now other students are becoming part of the conflict just because they are members of those cliques. The "jocks" have been joking about "cleaning up the school," a reference to the fact that kids in the alternative group (we call ourselves "worms") do not dress very neatly. And on the wall of this boy Matthew's house, a place where many of the "jocks" hang out, there was graffiti last week that said: "Kill a Jock for Jesus." (Matthew's parents are serious Christians and are trying to sue the school or something because of this.) This stupid stuff goes on even though most of us grew up in Yorkville and have known each other since elementary school.

Over the past couple of months there have been a number of near fights, and one real fight three weeks ago at a party. The police got involved the last time because a boy named Ethan badly hurt one of Billie's friends named Gomez. Ethan and Gomez haven't liked each other since they were little kids. Now they have to go to court because both of their parents filed charges. Everyone has been upset about this, and accusations have been going around.

Then last Thursday, in front of school, someone shouted "Hey Nigger!" to Garfield, this African-American kid. Garfield couldn't figure out who said it. Even though they aren't really friends, when Billie heard about this, he got all of his friends together to stick up for Garfield. (Billie has got a big heart like that.) Over the weekend there were cars full of angry kids cruising the streets looking for a fight—Billie's friends in some, Nate's in others. Fortunately there was no actual confrontation, but Tony (a friend of Nate's and the school basketball star) got his car windshield broken by a rock. No one knows who did it, but rumor is that it was Danielle. Danielle is Billie's cousin. She is only in eighth grade.

In school on Monday there were rumors that a fight was going down at this field after school. About 60 kids were supposedly going to show up. Nate's girlfriend, Jolie, who is always ready for a fight, was barking about it all day. The principal, Ms. Aramian, found out about the situation and asked the school's mediation program to get involved.

Major Parties in the Yorkville High Conflict
The "Worms":

Christine (Caucasian), girlfriend of Billie, sister of Nate. She is one of the central parties in the conflict.

Billie (Cape Verdean), Christine's boyfriend. He was initially harassed by Nate, and along with his friends has harassed Nate and his friends back.

Garfield (African-American), an acquaintance of Billie's. He overheard an unidentified person shout a racial epithet on school grounds. Billie and his friends came to Garfield's defense.

Gomez (Latino), a friend of Billie's. He was involved in a serious fight with Ethan for which he has to go to court.

Danielle (Caucasian), Billie's eighth grade cousin. She allegedly broke Tony's windshield.

The "Jocks":

Nate (Caucasian), Christine's brother. He has been harassing Christine and her boyfriend Billie because the latter is Cape Verdean.

Frank (Caucasian), a friend of Nate's. He self-identifies as a skin-head and is openly racist. He harasses Billie and his friends.

Matthew (Caucasian and Christian), a friend of Nate's and the others. The "jock" group often hangs out at Matthew's house, where someone (allegedly one of the "worms") wrote "Kill a Jock for Jesus" on the wall.

Ethan (Caucasian), a friend of Nate's and the others. He was involved in a serious fight with Billie's friend Gomez that resulted in police and court involvement.

Tony (Caucasian), a friend of Nate's and a school basketball star. The windshield of his car was broken over the weekend, allegedly by Danielle.

Jolie (Caucasian), Nate's girlfriend. She was encouraging people to fight after school.

Others:
Robert Melhoon (Caucasian), peer mediation coordinator.
Sandra Joyce (Caucasian), mediator and trainer from the
  Yorkville community asked to mediate the dispute.
Randy West (African-American), 12th grade student medi-
  ator asked to co-mediate with Sandra.
Janet Aramian (Caucasian), Yorkville High School princi-
  pal and strong supporter of the mediation effort.
Roy Johnson (African-American), school counselor and
  track coach asked to participate in the process as a support person for the students.
Joy Chin (Asian-American), co-coordinator of the mediation program with Robert Melhoon, sitting in on the
  sessions to support the mediation team.

The large group mediation process can be divided into the following
four phases:

1. Garnering Support for Mediation
2. Assessment, Preparation and Preliminary Private Sessions
3. Joint Sessions
4. Follow-Up

Bear in mind that although dividing mediation into phases is helpful for
learning purposes, it is an artificial division. In real life, there is a great deal
of chronological overlap.

Phase I: Garnering Support for Mediation

Before deciding whether to mediate a large group dispute, coordinators
must ensure that they have the support necessary to do so effectively. There
are three kinds of support to consider: administrative support, skilled mediators, and assistance from school staff and community members. If even
one of these is lacking, it can be difficult and even potentially dangerous to
mediate some large group disputes.

1. Administrative Support.

School administrators must unequivocally support efforts to mediate a particular large group dispute.[*] They alone can provide the flexibility necessary to make the process work within the school environment of bells and passes. From the start, inform administrators about what is needed to manage a case successfully. The list includes:

- Three to ten times the amount of time—in the form of intake, preparation, actual joint and private sessions, and follow-up—needed for disputes involving two parties. A mediator or coordinator might devote many school days to resolving one large group conflict.
- Substantial assistance from school staff, who of necessity will miss their usual responsibilities.
- The ability to pull participants (both parties and mediators) out of class according to the unique and unforeseen dynamics of each dispute.
- Pro-active and constructive efforts to address teachers' possible opposition to the process.
- Additional space in which to conduct the sessions.
- Administrators' best efforts to ensure that any intervention they make into the dispute is *separate* from, and does not have a negative impact upon, the mediation process.
- Willingness to seriously consider supporting any resolution created by the parties.

At the same time that mediators are requesting this latitude, they also need to minimize administrators' expectations. Experience with a wide range of large group disputes demonstrates that if mediators have the necessary support, and if a critical mass of parties choose to participate, the process will be extremely beneficial. But there is never a guarantee that mediation will make a conflict better, and it could even make it worse.

---

[*] On occasion, the coordinator and even the mediator may *be* an administrator.

Administrators themselves sometimes require that certain people participate in the process for safety or liability issues. This issue must be discussed until everyone feels comfortable. Under certain circumstances, coordinators may also invite school administrators to sit in on the mediation session. Administrators can be asked to participate in the entire process *as parties* who must follow the rules of mediation, or as school representatives who express support for parties' efforts at the start of the session and then leave. This latter strategy impresses upon disputants both the importance of the process and the fact that it is in their control. Its usefulness depends upon how parties perceive the particular administrator.

Do not assume that administrators who have championed efforts to mediate interpersonal disputes will necessarily support efforts to mediate a large group dispute. Large group disputes put administrators in the center of a storm. Tremendous pressure is exerted upon them to act in a timely and effective manner from within and outside the school. To ensure their support, meet with administrators early, carefully review everyone's expectations, and obtain their commitment to the process.

> *The mediators in the Yorkville High School dispute were lucky: Janet Aramian, the principal, was very supportive of their efforts. Ms. Aramian had participated in a mediation training at her previous school, and she was instrumental in establishing a peer mediation program at Yorkville High. She and the mediation coordinator agreed that because of a history of strained relations with a number of the parties, she would keep her distance from the mediation.*

2. Skilled Mediators.

The normal stresses and challenges of mediating are exacerbated in large group mediations. The potential for things to go wrong is much greater, and no matter how well one plans, to a large extent these mediation sessions must be improvised. It is therefore essential to utilize mediators who have the ability to meet these challenges. Although experienced student mediators (especially at the high school level) have demonstrated that they can mediate large group conflicts, adults are generally more involved either as mediators or as support people. In the most difficult cases, at least one of the mediators should be an experienced adult.

Sometimes student mediators are concerned about the repercussions of mediating a large group dispute. It might also be difficult to find a mediator within school, student or adult, whom all parties will perceive as impartial. In these cases, look outside the school to find mediators. Contact training sources, local mediation programs, universities, or any other resource that can help locate mediators. These groups will often provide mediators, offer technical assistance, help coordinate sessions, and provide much needed moral support. (Experienced mediators are usually excited by the prospect of being involved in a complex, large group dispute.) When community mediators are invited to work within the school, arrange for less experienced, school-based mediators to "shadow" them and build the school's capacity to mediate these disputes in the future. Remember: School-based mediators do not have to do this alone.

> *When Ms. Aramian requested assistance from the mediation program, the mediation coordinator, Robert Melhoon, decided to ask an experienced community mediator for help. The first person he thought of was Sandra Joyce, a mediator who had helped train the school's student mediators. Robert and Sandra together decided that Randy West, a 12th grade student, would co-mediate the dispute with Sandra. This gave them gender balance, a student voice on the mediation team, and because Randy was African-American and Sandra was white, the racial diversity that was essential for this case.*

3. The Assistance of School Staff and Community Members.

Regardless of how many parties are involved in a large group mediation, schools usually use the same number of mediators (in most cases, two) that they normally use. But there are many ways that others can assist in this application of the mediation process. The time consuming work of coordinating these cases, as well as other work that is unique to large group disputes, can be done by those willing to support the effort.

Each dispute will require different types and degrees of assistance. The categories of help that supporters and "assistant" coordinators may provide include:

- **Logistical Support.** This includes a wide range of activities. Supportive adults can help locate parties, conduct intake interviews, encourage parties to try mediation, escort parties to sessions, convene sessions, coordinate/mediate other disputes that arise while the large group process is underway, sit with parties during private sessions, and serve as an emissary to student parties' parents. In some cases supporters have acted as "security advisors," standing near exits and outside rooms to prevent interruptions. In one large mediation that involved cafeteria workers as parties, supporters chopped vegetables to enable these staff members to attend the sessions.[*]

- **Support for Parties.** Because of the constraints of their role, sometimes mediators cannot speak with parties as forthrightly as can other students and adults whom the parties respect. It therefore can be helpful to invite adults whom parties trust to observe the mediation process. These individuals act as allies of both the *process* and the *parties,* encouraging groups to participate fully, making sure they get their needs met, and listening to parties' concerns between sessions. They can serve as "ground rule monitors" if parties are acting inappropriately. During the breaks in a session, they can tell a party in private: "Nate, you are smarter than this! If you don't straighten this thing out, I fear you're going to get kicked out of school." These support people also add a degree of safety and respectability to the process.

THERE IS NO EDUCATION LIKE ADVERSITY.
BENJAMIN DISRAELI

Large Groups

---

[*] In a number of cases in Massachusetts, as many as a dozen volunteer community mediators have gone to a school to conduct individual intake interviews with each party in a large group dispute. With each interview taking thirty to forty five minutes, and possibly fifty parties involved in a conflict, it is easy to understand why outside support can be invaluable.

- **Support for Mediators.** Supportive adults sometimes observe the mediation process solely to help the *mediators*. Though they never speak directly to parties, these support people work as a team with mediators and coordinators, meeting before and after each session to share ideas and plan for the work ahead. Support staff commonly see or hear cues that the mediators miss. Those who know parties offer insights into their personalities and the character of the dispute. They can also give mediators feedback to help them improve their skills. Of course, supporters must uphold the same level of confidentiality as the mediators and respect their position relative to the parties.

- **Follow-up Support.** Adults who have attended the mediation sessions may help with follow-up as well. They enable the mediation effort to maintain contact with large numbers of parties in a way that would be impossible for a single coordinator or mediator.

- **Interpretation.** When individuals or groups speak a different first language, support staff can assist with interpretation.*

A variety of individuals may assume supportive roles during a large group mediation. Mediation coordinators and other adults trained as mediators are the obvious first choice (one of many reasons to train school staff to be mediators). Also enlist the aid of teachers, school social workers and counselors, as well as allies from the community such as community mediators, youth workers, D.A.R.E. officers, gang specialists and other civic leaders. When inviting members of the community into school, it is always advisable to make sure this is acceptable with administrators.

Mediators and coordinators must take a number of actions when utilizing additional support people in a large group dispute. The most essential is to make sure that parties feel comfortable with the individuals and the role

---

* See Chapter 10 for more information on using interpreters in mediation.

they will play during the process. Solicit groups' feelings during preliminary private sessions and again when they meet face-to-face. If parties are uncomfortable with any potential support person, reconsider using them. Deferring to parties reinforces that they are in charge and avoids problems down the road.

It is equally important that support personnel understand their role in the process. If they are only observing the session, they should refrain from commenting on the issues being discussed and defer to the parties and mediators. When they are asked to participate as parties, supportive adults should not expect preferential treatment because of their age or position. They should also avoid "lecturing" student parties. If support people are uncomfortable with these constraints, or if mediators feel they will have difficulty abiding by them, then do not include these adults in the session.

A word of caution: Logistical mix-ups and misunderstandings are more likely as the number of people involved in the process increases. Parties have been told that sessions were to start at different times or that mediators want to meet with them for an hour when in fact it was for three hours. Be careful to make sure that everyone is working with the same information.

Finally, remember that mediation is a private process. Think carefully before inviting people to participate, and invite only those who will truly contribute. Utilizing support people can make the difficult process of mediating large group disputes a good deal easier. Experienced coordinators identify them as soon as they start working on a case.

Mr. Melhoon asked a number of people for assistance. He first turned to the team of teachers that assisted him as coordinator. These educators would co-coordinate and help with all of the logistics. (One of them, Joy Chin, was also going to observe the sessions to support the mediators.) Roy Johnson, one of the school's counselors and the track coach, was another person Mr. Melhoon asked to help. The mediation team felt that Roy, an

African-American and trusted confidant of all students but most especially of the students of color, would be a very helpful addition to the process. Roy was to be a support person for students. (Significantly, Roy also happened to have a positive relationship with Nate, who ran cross country.) Finally, the mediation team asked three student mediators to be available to assist with logistics such as setting up chairs, escorting parties back to class, copying paperwork, etc.

Time pressure usually necessitates that coordinators complete the bulk of the support building work within 48 hours of receiving the initial referral. Once the administration has given its blessings, skilled mediators have signed on, and support staff are in place, coordinators have the fundamentals necessary to begin the work of the next phase.

Phase II: Assessment, Preparation, and Preliminary Private Sessions

When mediating large group disputes, extensive assessment and preparatory work lays the foundation for successful face-to-face sessions. Without this work, it is likely that joint sessions will disintegrate and agreements that are created will be ineffective. The intensity of this phase represents one of the biggest differences between large group disputes and two-party disputes, where mediators with only a thumbnail sketch of a conflict often conduct a joint session immediately following intake. Perhaps the most striking feature of this phase is the use of preliminary private sessions.

FAILURE TO PREPARE IS PREPARING TO FAIL.

JOHN WOODEN

The following sections discuss the goals and strategies utilized during this second important stage of large group work.

Preliminary Private Sessions or Joint Session?

When the number of parties involved in a dispute soars, mediators apply a unique degree of creative control over the structure of the mediation process.

Large Groups

Whether to meet with disputing groups together or separately is a crucial concern in this regard. Complicating matters is that at the start of most large group mediations, the stakes appear very high. Mediators may not know the parties or their dispute very well, and there is often a sense of urgency among administrators, parents, and even the parties. Coordinators and mediators do not have the luxury of a great deal of time to analyze the situation.

Most mediators choose to begin with what can be called "preliminary private sessions." A preliminary private session is essentially a meeting with a single constituency or group member conducted *prior to* the joint session. The reasons behind the decision to begin with preliminary private sessions are:

1. Not knowing the specifics of the dispute, it is too risky for both the success of the process and the safety of the parties to meet face-to-face initially. With so much potential for parties to inflame one another—and for chaos and even violence to result—it is best to enable parties to "vent" in private.

2. Mediators need to win the trust of the parties, and parties are more likely to have their guard down during private sessions.

3. Mediators are better able to gather information about a dispute, including identifying additional parties, in the relative safety of a private session. Parties' posturing is too great in early joint sessions, and they might not be completely open in front of their adversaries.

4. Parties must abide by appropriate rules of conduct if mediation is to work, and it is much easier to get their commitment to such rules in a private than in a joint session.

There *are* reasons that argue for initially meeting with parties in a joint session, however. The most compelling is that a joint session concretely demonstrates to parties that the resolution process has begun. When groups first meet in private sessions, their feelings of self-righteousness and solidarity may increase. Later, they might hear rumors about what their adversaries said in their private meeting. In some instances, this has led to the escalation of a conflict prior to the joint session.[*] By simply observing the other group in the room during the initial joint session, parties get the message that their adversaries want to "work things out." This can result in an implicit agreement between groups that minimizes the chances of escalation and bodes well for the resolution process. Another important reason to hold a joint session first is simply that private sessions are unnecessary because the conflict is not very volatile.

Like so many aspects of mediating, then, compelling factors may argue for opposing courses of action. Mediators have devised some creative approaches to address this tension. One is to conduct a very brief joint session to initiate the process and then move to private sessions. This demonstrates parties' willingness to resolve the conflict and builds their confidence in the process and in the mediators. Observing groups interact also provides mediators with a valuable reading on the tone of the dispute. A second approach is to conduct a series of brief joint sessions with smaller, rotating teams of representatives from all sides of a dispute (so that every party attends one of these joint sessions). This also signifies to parties that the process is underway, and limiting the size of the groups minimizes the risks associated with initial joint sessions. This is very effective for conflicts that involve a large percentage of a school community (racial tensions, controversial changes in school policy, etc.).

Mediators determine whether to begin with private or joint sessions on a case-by-case basis. In addition to the factors just discussed, other considerations include the degree of security personnel needed and available for an initial joint session, and the relationship mediators have with the parties. If the process can be kept compact, however, without many days separating the early sessions, consider beginning with preliminary private sessions.

In the Yorkville dispute, Robert Melhoon had to act quickly. The

---

* One of the only deaths tangentially associated with a mediation process this author knows about occurred when the mediators began with private sessions in a gang-related dispute, the parties got emotional, and a student party was murdered in the community before mediators had the opportunity to bring the groups together.

*case was referred to him at 11:30 a.m. on a Monday, and the
fight was to take place that afternoon. After arranging for
Sandra and Randy to mediate the following day, he and his co-
coordinators decided to meet individually with as many parties
as they could locate. By the end of the school day they had met
with approximately 25 students, sometimes with two or three
people from the same side simultaneously. In addition, two students were interviewed by phone at their work/study place-
ments. The meetings were brief, generally about ten minutes.
The coordinators listened to the students' concerns, explained the
mediation process, and then asked:*

1. *Will you attend a meeting, to be held tomorrow morning in the conference room, and tell your whole story to
a team of mediators? Only people on your side of the
dispute will attend.*
2. *Will you agree to call off the fight today and avoid the
other group members until that time?*

*With varying degrees of enthusiasm, all students agreed and said
they would inform their friends about the meetings the next day.
At Mr. Melhoon's suggestion, Billie and Christine agreed to be
escorted to home and work respectively after school. Extra security personnel were stationed outside of school at the end of the
day, and the Yorkville police were alerted to patrol the field
where the fight was to be held.*

Identifying, Gathering, and Interviewing the Parties

When a conflict involving just two parties is referred to mediation, coordinators need not concern themselves with identifying the parties—both
names are provided for them. But when large group conflicts are referred,
the coordinator is initially faced with a unique problem: determining who is
a party to the conflict. Because large group conflicts usually involve loosely
affiliated sets of students, there is no quick list that can be checked. And it
is important to include all parties to the conflict or the mediation process
can not be completely effective.

Unfortunately, there is no easy formula for identifying parties. Begin by interviewing parties who *have been* referred; they will volunteer the names of still other parties who may be involved. In addition, regard any person who is even remotely connected to the dispute as a potential lead. Large group conflicts are usually very public affairs, and important information can be discovered through unexpected sources. Experienced coordinators know that individuals who were not involved in the particular incident that brought a conflict to light may still be integral parties to the larger, ongoing dispute.

If a dispute appears to involve twenty individuals or less, it may be possible to identify them, conduct an *individual* intake interview with each one, and proceed accordingly. Though not always necessary, this one-to-one contact with each party can only benefit the effort. When the conflict is larger, however, it may be too time consuming and logistically impossible to locate and speak with each party individually. In these cases, mediators and coordinators hold separate, private meetings for each *group.* All parties who are affiliated with a particular group are invited to attend. The meetings can be advertised through public announcement or word of mouth.

When assembling parties for such meetings, consider this: Attending a private meeting with one's allies is not a big risk. Potential benefits to parties include that preliminary private sessions give them the opportunity to learn from their allies about what has happened. (Even members of the same group are rarely all together to discuss the situation.) Parties also lose nothing and are under no obligation to continue in the mediation process by attending the initial meeting. Convince the leaders of a group to attend, and usually the rest will follow. If parties are treated with respect, chances are good that they will welcome the opportunity, as well as the attention, and will choose to attend the meeting.

A final note on identifying parties: Be prepared for the number of parties involved in large group mediations to expand and contract during the early stages of the process. Those who attend the initial meeting but do not have an emotional investment in the conflict should not be asked to return once the process begins in earnest. Others, who hesitated to become involved at the outset, will decide to participate in later sessions after they hear good things about mediation from their friends. Although this can be difficult on the mediators—those who become involved at a later stage of the process may not have "reconciled" as much as those who were there from the start— it is often unavoidable. Prevent parties who join the process from hindering the groups' progress by preparing them during intake and encouraging them to speak with their allies.

Some mediators, because of personal style or because of their understanding of what is best for a particular dispute, are inflexible about this issue and will not allow the number of participants to fluctuate. Either way, the numbers should stabilize as the joint session approaches.

> *At Yorkville, meetings were held with the two groups at 8:00 a.m. and 10:30 a.m. on Tuesday, the day after the initial referral. Rather than call themselves the "black" group, which they found inaccurate as well as offensive, Christine, Billie and their friends preferred the designation "worms," a name they used affectionately to refer to themselves. The other group referred to themselves as "jocks." Forty-eight students attended the "worms" meeting, eighty percent of whom were people of color. Twenty-five Caucasian students attended the "jock" meeting, all but three of whom were male. Twenty minutes into this latter meeting, two other students, Tony and Ethan, were located and joined the group.*

> *Danielle, the middle school student, was not able to attend because her principal did not allow her to leave school grounds.*

Parent Involvement in Large Group Disputes

Because of the serious nature of many large group disputes involving students, parents often learn of them from their own children, from the parents of other children, from the school, and even from the community press.

Sometimes a dispute between groups of students causes related but wholly separate disputes among parents and between parents and the school. Coordinators and mediators, therefore, working in conjunction with school administrators, often meet with parents to address their concerns and solicit their assistance in resolving large group disputes involving students.

Most mediators will not include parents in the actual mediation sessions, however. Their fundamental reason is that mediators discourage the participation of individuals who are not a direct party to a dispute. There are also other reasons to exclude parents, including that:

- Parents' presence often inhibits students and makes them less likely to tell the whole story and accept responsibility for their part in a conflict.
- Parents may have difficulty controlling themselves. Even when they have been asked to observe quietly, parents sometimes intervene to defend their child or impugn someone else's.
- Parents are sometimes more interested in "fighting it out" than students, holding on to the promise of retribution long after their children are ready to make amends.

Although parents may become upset if they are not included in the session, usually they understand that the conflict can be resolved satisfactorily without them. Of course, parents can always prohibit their child from participating in mediation.

Large group mediation sessions *have been* conducted with parents in attendance. In one case, a meeting was held with parents prior to the session during which they agreed to be observers and let students speak for themselves and make their own decisions. In another, parents were encouraged to express their thoughts and feelings both at the start and at the conclusion of a joint session, but they remained quiet during the bulk of the session. Watching one's children mediate can be a powerful experience for parents and have a positive impact upon their lives at home.[*] Mediators have also

---

[*] One school reported an unexpected benefit of allowing parents to participate in a large group mediation session. In this particular middle school, as is true in far too many schools in North America, there had been a disturbing lack of parent involvement in school life. Participating

conducted separate mediation sessions for parents prior to, during, and after they have addressed the student dispute.

When parents are truly parties to a dispute, they should certainly be included in a session. But in general, although parents can be involved in a support capacity, it is inadvisable to include them in the actual mediation sessions with their children.

> *In Yorkville, parents of many of the student parties were unaware of the problem. Although the graffiti on Matthew's home had been featured in the local papers, the larger story of how this and the other incidents fit together was not well known. (Earlier in the year, Christine Jones had asked a school adjustment counselor to meet with her mother, Ruth, but her mother never responded.) The mediators, along with Mr. Melhoon, decided not to contact parents regarding this dispute. Parents who did call the school were apprised of the situation and informed that they would be invited to a follow-up meeting along with all of the parties' parents. (Parents were aware of the school's mediation program because Mr. Melhoon had sent a letter in September informing them about the program and giving them the option to prevent their child from participating. Only three parents—none of the parents of the students involved in this dispute—had chosen this option.)*

The First Meeting: Group Intake Interview or Preliminary Private Session?

If one decides to conduct an initial meeting with each group, another subtle but critical question must be answered: Is the meeting going to be an intake interview, a preliminary private session, or both? In disputes between two parties, the *coordinator* usually conducts an intake interview with each party. The primary goal of this interview is to assess whether the conflict is appro-

in the mediation process got parents talking to one another, and not only about the dispute at hand. They discovered that they shared many concerns for their children, and in the end they formed a parent group.   Their first goal: Move school bus stops away from drug-infested areas of their neighborhood.

priate for mediation and determine whether parties are willing to participate in the process. If they are, then a mediation session is scheduled at a later time with *mediators*.

But in large group mediations, if the initial meetings are conducted as intake interviews, and if parties decide to mediate, then the coordinator may have to reconvene the same people in the same format for a preliminary private session. This is no small task given the logistical obstacles to assembling large numbers of parties during the school day. For this and other reasons, coordinators often combine the intake interview and the preliminary private session during large group mediations.

The availability of mediators is key to determining whether this is possible. While intake interviews are conducted by the coordinator, preliminary private sessions *must be conducted by those who will be mediating the dispute*. A great deal can be accomplished during these private sessions, from trust building to information gathering to agenda setting. It is therefore essential that mediators facilitate them.

When group intake interviews and preliminary private sessions are combined, one follows directly upon the heels of the other. Mediators may conduct the intake interview themselves, or they may do so in collaboration with the coordinator (who in some instances might be one of the mediators). Although there is a seamlessness that prevents the uninformed from noticing the distinction, the two portions of the meeting have different goals.

Group Intake Interviews

The goals of *group* intake interviews are similar to those of *individual* intake interviews.[29] During group intake interviews, coordinators:

- Introduce the mediation process.
- Build parties' trust in the mediation program.
- Determine the nature of the conflict. (How do parties perceive the situation? What are the issues? What is the relationship of the

parties? How urgently does the situation need attention?)
- Determine whether the conflict is appropriate for mediation. (Are
  there identifiable parties? Is there potential for violence? Are there
  negotiable issues? Are parties capable of making age-appropriate
  commitments? Can the conflict be resolved without mediation?)
- Encourage parties to try mediation if their conflict seems
  appropriate.
- Refer parties to other people and programs that might be of
  assistance.

Parties to large group disputes sometimes will not commit themselves to
mediation individually. The group intake interview provides the opportunity to meet with friends and allies and decide how to proceed *as a group*. As
always, they may still choose not to participate in mediation. The dynamics
of group interaction, especially among young people, can magnify their
bravado and make them less likely to choose mediation. Parties may not
want to give up the benefits (prestige, attention, peer support, excitement)
that accrue to them as a result of the conflict. It may not even be in the
legitimate best interests of the group to mediate. In these cases, especially if
there is concern about further trouble between groups, coordinators refer the
situation back to school administrators.

Even when parties choose *not to* mediate, however, the group intake interview may be beneficial to them. During the interview, parties clear up misunderstandings and rumors associated with the dispute. They express their
thoughts and arrive at new insights about the situation. Student parties feel
respected and listened to by the school, something they might not feel very
often. Though it may not resolve all of the issues in dispute, simply participating in the intake interview can end the intimidation and escalating violence between groups.

Many groups come to perceive that mediation is in their best interest, even
if they are initially skeptical. Parties grow to trust the mediators and their

Large Groups

unfamiliar process, and their natural curiosity makes them want to give it a try. Often those who want to mediate convince others who do not. And at this point, the preliminary private session begins.

Preliminary Private Sessions

Preliminary private sessions mark the beginning of the formal large group mediation. Many aspects of the practice and goals of these meetings are unique to the large group process. In preliminary private sessions, mediators:

- **Explore issues in depth.** This includes uncovering the true interests and feelings of the parties, finding out which issues are most important to them, and determining what concessions parties might be willing to "give" to the other group.

- **Become familiar with the character of each group.** When people are in groups, they can behave differently than they do individually. Mediators must become familiar with the unique dynamics of each group. By asking parties directly and through observation, mediators attempt to answer the following questions:

  —Which parties function in a leadership capacity within a group?

  —Which parties are supportive of conciliation efforts?

  —Which parties might try to sabotage the mediation process (and would benefit from a private meeting with the mediators)?

  —What alliances, coalitions, or cliques exist within each group and between members of opposing groups?

  —Which individuals are involved in a clearly defined interpersonal conflict with individuals from their own or other groups?

- **Encourage intra-group communication.** It is quite common for parties on the same side of a dispute to have partial information and competing versions of events. Mediators encourage parties to talk to one another about their experience of the conflict in order to eliminate misunderstandings. It is much easier to learn new information from each other than from members of opposing groups.

And informed parties are generally the easiest to work with.

- **Explore the feasibility of joint sessions.** While observing the behavior of a group in the preliminary private session, mediators hope to determine whether it would be possible and wise to bring groups together, and if so, in what form.
- **Prepare parties for joint sessions.** Mediators help parties identify their common interests and sometimes even have them practice presenting their concerns to the other parties.
- **Choose spokespeople.** If mediators decide to use spokespeople (more on this below), then the preliminary private session is an appropriate time to choose them and explore how to utilize them (for example, deciding when spokespeople will report back to their constituencies).

Some mediators write a summary of each group's concerns and distribute it to the parties after preliminary private sessions. This demonstrates the mediators' attentiveness and it enables parties to correct any inaccuracies. The document also helps mediators fashion an agenda for future sessions. One concern with this approach, however, is that with so many copies available, it becomes difficult to maintain parties' privacy.

A final caution when parties are young people: Being among a group of angry and vulnerable peers can accentuate students' tendency to be rude and anti-social. This is especially true if they have not yet come to trust the mediators. Parties may verbally attack mediators so skillfully that they severely test the latter's ability to be non-defensive. Adult mediators who fall into a pejorative, "stop that behavior this minute" tone when faced with student criticism guarantee that the mediation effort will fail. Instead, mediators should acknowledge parties' anger but stand up for the process and for their right to be respected in an assertive and non-accusatory way. ("I understand how upsetting this is to everyone, but there is no need to attack us. We are just here to help.") Enlisting the support of people that students know and respect from the start is one way to minimize this problem.

Large Groups

A PROBLEM WELL STATED IS A PROBLEM HALF SOLVED.

CHARLES F. KETTERING

Large Groups

*Preliminary private sessions at Yorkville High were very con-
structive, and both sides expressed an interest in continuing with
mediation. In the first meeting with the "worms," Christine
spoke through tears about how things were out of control and she
was so embarrassed by her brother. Billie said that he was only
defending himself; if Nate hadn't started the whole thing then
there would be no problem. Gomez said very little, and Garfield
explained that the racism he experienced wasn't only from kids at
the high school, but from the teachers and the community as well.
One third of the 48 students attending had not been involved in
the group conflict but came solely to express their concern about
racism in the school.*

*In the second meeting for the "jocks," most of the students were
friends and expressed that they were just sticking up for each
other. A few complained that the "black" kids defaced public
property and called them "crackers" and other negative names.
Nate said he just didn't like Billie (who he called a "sleaze") and
that his sister Christine should stick to her own kind. Frank's
blatant racism ("I don't like black people, period!") amused Nate,
Matthew and some others, but a few parties, most notably
Ethan, distanced themselves from Frank. Ethan said that a
person's skin color was not an issue for him, that he had not
planned on fighting yesterday, and that he thought Frank was
stupid. (With his court date impending, he appeared genuinely
mature and circumspect.) Tony, with apologies, told Nate that
maybe he should leave his sister alone and let her live her own
life. He just wanted to find out who busted his windshield and
then forget the whole thing.*

Identify and Attend to Discrete Interpersonal Disputes

Almost all large group disputes have interpersonal conflicts tangled within
them, conflicts that usually serve as the catalyst for the larger dispute.
Typically, rumors and allegations lead friends of those involved in the smaller conflicts to join in. These friends take actions that escalate the situation
and lead still other people to become involved. Eventually a critical mass is

reached and the situation erupts into what is recognizable as the large group conflict.

Even though the number of parties involved in the conflict grows, the discrete interpersonal conflicts at its center remain intact. Some of these may be relatively minor disputes, and the parties in question will quickly forget them once the large group conflict is resolved. For the more serious interpersonal conflicts, however, it is essential that mediators also work with parties to those disputes independently of the large group.

When individuals are able to resolve their discrete interpersonal conflicts, it can benefit the effort to settle the larger dispute. This is especially true if the parties are well-respected within their groups. Once these disputants make peace, it demonstrates to their constituencies that reconciliation is possible and can create a momentum towards resolution. In contrast, if these interpersonal conflicts are not resolved, then even when group tensions are reduced there remains the possibility that an interpersonal problem will re-ignite the larger dispute.

Identify discrete interpersonal disputes by asking the parties, the referral source and others who are familiar with the conflict: "Do you/does he have a long-standing conflict with any person on the other side?" Interpersonal conflicts can also be uncovered by observing individuals and groups interact during intake and preliminary private sessions. Although these avenues usually identify most of these conflicts, be prepared to discover others even into the joint sessions.

After identifying discrete interpersonal tensions within a large group dispute, mediators then decide whether it is important to mediate them separately. Will these smaller disputes fade as tensions diminish between groups, or will they persist regardless? Use the following criteria to help make this determination. If even one of these criteria is present, consider mediating the conflict separately.

> NINE-TENTHS OF THE SERIOUS CONTROVERSIES WHICH ARISE IN LIFE RESULT FROM MISUNDERSTANDING.
>
> LOUIS BRANDEIS

Large Groups

Large Groups

1. The conflict has its own unique and extensive history (although it intersects with the chronology of the larger dispute).
2. The conflict involves issues that directly affect only the parties in question.
3. The parties have strong negative and unresolved feelings directed specifically towards one another.
4. The conflict appears to be preventing key disputants and their supporters from resolving the large group dispute.

If mediators do attempt to work with an interpersonal conflict separately, the next question to answer is *when*? In general, strive to conduct these separate sessions *as early in the process as possible*. Ideally, mediators help parties resolve these discrete interpersonal disputes while intake and preliminary private sessions are underway. But often parties prefer to wait until after the joint sessions have started and groups meet face-to-face. Once parties feel comfortable with the mediators and the mediation process, and once they learn additional information about the dispute during the joint session, they may be more likely to agree to mediate their discrete interpersonal disputes.

After joint sessions have begun, there are still a number of options for mediating interpersonal disputes:

- **Mediate during the joint session.** Although tempting, it is very difficult to mediate an interpersonal dispute while parties' peers are present. Disputants feel too much pressure to "maintain face." True private sessions are also impossible. An alternative is to mediate discrete interpersonal conflicts in a separate room while the large group session continues. Of course, it is necessary to have extra mediators available (the coordinator?) to do this. The fact that the parties in question would miss the joint session does not make this option very appealing.
- **Mediate in between joint sessions.** Because there may be multiple joint sessions in large group disputes, mediating the smaller disputes

between sessions is a wonderful option if the parties are willing.

- **Mediate after the large group conflict is resolved.** This is most common because parties often do not agree to participate until this time. Once the large group dispute has dissipated, it sets in relief the interpersonal tensions that remain.

Whenever discrete interpersonal disputes are resolved separately, remember to help parties decide how to present the results of their private discussions to their peers. Perhaps they would like to speak with friends and allies in private. Or simply telling peers informally that "everything is OK" might be adequate. When a discrete interpersonal dispute was a central issue in the larger conflict, consider asking parties to discuss their progress during a joint session with everyone in attendance. Often these disputants will *want* to offer assistance as peacemakers/mediators; this can be valuable boost to the large group effort.

Regardless of when discrete interpersonal disputes are mediated and how parties present their progress to their constituencies, it will be time well spent.

> *In Yorkville, the mediators identified a number of discrete interpersonal disputes, most notably between Nate and Christine, Nate and Billie, and Ethan and Gomez. The team felt that the interpersonal disputes involving Nate were most closely entwined with the large group dispute, and Mr. Melhoon arranged to meet with him immediately following the preliminary private session. They were disappointed when Nate refused to meet with any party individually (including his sister) until after the large group sessions had concluded.*

> *Since Ethan seemed so conciliatory during the preliminary private session with the "jocks," at its conclusion the mediators asked him whether he would like to mediate with Gomez in private. Ethan enthusiastically agreed. Gomez was contacted late Tuesday afternoon and he also agreed. Mr. Melhoon asked both students to request their parents' permission because of the pend-*

ing court actions. On Wednesday they informed him that their parents had consented in writing, and a session was scheduled for Thursday, the day before the large group joint session.

On the advice of the police and parents, Gomez and Ethan had not spoken to one another since the fight. At the start of the session, Ethan immediately apologized to Gomez. As their conversation progressed, the two discussed how tensions between them had started with a conflict over a girlfriend in 5th grade! Rumors and allegations had fueled their discord ever since. Gomez mentioned that he and Ethan had been friends for most of elementary school, and had even gone over each other's houses to play. The two left the session on good terms, committed to speaking with their friends about what Ethan called the "insanity" of the current group conflict.

Formalize the Agreement to Participate

In large group disputes, getting parties' commitment to participate in mediation is more challenging. Not only are there more parties, but disputants on the same side of the dispute can disagree about whether to try mediation. Although mediation sessions can be conducted with only a portion of the members of a group, it is preferable to have *all* members involved. This is especially true when organized groups like gangs or sports teams are involved and students that refuse to participate in mediation could undermine the progress made by those that do.

LISTENING IS A MAGNETIC AND STRANGE THING, A CREATIVE FORCE.

KARL MENNINGER

In addition, the fact that large group disputes can take days or even weeks to mediate requires a greater degree of commitment from participants. There is an unavoidable period of time in which the conflict resolution process is underway but the conflict has not been resolved. If parties act in a way that escalates the conflict during this time, it can effectively destroy the mediation effort. Parties' agreement to abide by the ground rules of mediation must therefore extend for the duration of the mediation process.

Large Groups

Many coordinators and mediators manage these challenges by formalizing the "agreement to participate" parties make with the mediation program. These agreements are the equivalent of "cease-fires" or truces, in which parties resolve to maintain peaceful relations with each other until the mediation process is complete. Once these agreements are accepted, written down, and signed, all participants are assured that there will be no escalation of the conflict while the mediation is underway.

Consider including generic points like the following in an agreement to participate:

- Parties understand that they are participating voluntarily and can withdraw at any time.
- Parties agree to follow all of the ground rules of the mediation process (e.g., try to solve the problem, listen to each other, no interruptions, put-downs, name-calling or threats, no physical violence, etc.).
- Parties agree that for the duration of the mediation process, they will refrain from taking actions that in any way might escalate the conflict.
- Parties agree to minimize contact with members of other groups unless it is for positive purposes.
- Parties agree to attend all sessions.
- Parties agree to keep what happens in the sessions private until the mediation process is complete.
- Additional parties can attend only if all parties agree.

In addition to these requirements, mediators add points of agreement that are specific to the conflict at hand. Solicit input from the parties—they know best what will make the agreement to participate most effective. "Conflict-specific" examples might include:

—Parties agree not to make racial slurs.

—Parties agree to not carry any type of weapon to meetings.

—Parties agree to stay away from the window side of the cafeteria (disputed turf) until the conclusion of the mediation process.

Large Groups

Large Groups

—Parties agree to stay away from each other's neighborhoods until the situation is resolved.

As with all agreements, make sure this one is balanced, specific and realistic.

Mediators facilitate discussion within groups to build consensus concerning whether to "ratify" the agreement to participate. These discussions usually occur during preliminary private sessions, and the agreement to participate is formally approved either in those sessions or at the start of the first joint session. After mediators explain that when all group members participate, the likelihood of success increases, parties who want to participate often put pressure on and ultimately convince those who initially were unwilling. Mediators have been known to leave the room while parties decide whether to endorse an agreement to participate. As the first tangible agreement between groups, the acceptance of an agreement is an important step towards the resolution of a large group dispute.

A last note: It may be worthwhile to mediate a large group dispute even if a few parties choose not to participate. Tensions can be reduced and a greater understanding can be achieved as a result of discussions among those willing to mediate. The decision must be made on a case-by-case basis.

The agreement to participate was quite simple at Yorkville High. It included all of the generic points above and in addition, participants agreed to not make negative comments about other individuals and to stay away from each other's homes for the duration of the mediation. The joint session was scheduled for Friday of that week. Although mediators were concerned about the three day delay, scheduling problems made it unavoidable.

Control Who Will Speak Using Ground Rules and Spokespeople

When a dispute involves only two parties, determining *who* will speak in the mediation session is not an issue. With the mediators' guidance, both parties have the opportunity to say anything they feel is important about the dispute and about their relationship with the other party. This makes sense:

People resolve their own disputes only when they are given the opportunity to speak their minds.

As the number of parties in a dispute grows, however, mediators cannot take the issue of who will speak for granted. If everyone spoke in a session with thirty-five participants, it might take all day merely for parties to make their initial remarks.* Other problems are associated with having so many people speak, too. The process might disintegrate as parties lose their tempers, interrupt one another, and hurl accusations back and forth. Or the discussion might become redundant and make parties frustrated or bored. Mediators therefore usually take a unique degree of control over *who speaks* in large group mediations.

Mediators' goal here is to strike a balance between enabling all parties to participate in the process while maintaining as productive a discussion as possible. The most basic way to accomplish this is to create and enforce specific ground rules. Although using ground rules is a common feature of all mediation sessions, greater emphasis is placed upon these rules in large group disputes. They may be included in a formal "agreement to participate" and/or posted on the wall of the mediation room. Solicit parties' input when creating these rules. Common ground rules include:

- Speak as clearly as possible.
- Do not interrupt one another.
- No name-calling, put downs or threats.
- Try to add something new whenever possible rather then repeat what has already been said.
- Be as honest as you can.
- Stay within a five minute limit when necessary.

Sometimes ground rules alone are not enough to ensure that discussions run

---

* It is interesting to note that in cultures that have a more fluid conception of time (Native American cultures, for example), taking all day for the opening remarks in a large group dispute would not be perceived as a problem but rather as an essential and welcome part of the conflict resolution process. See Chapter 5 for further exploration of the impact of culture on mediation.

Large Groups

smoothly. In these cases, mediators employ an additional measure unique to large group disputes: spokespeople.

Using Spokespeople

Most times it is parties' presence at and direct participation in the mediation process that enables them to reconcile their differences. But in large group disputes, this ideal is sometimes impossible to achieve. Parties may be incapable of abiding by the ground rules necessary to create a safe environment for negotiations. Or the sheer number of parties may be unwieldy. There may not be an appropriate space to bring groups together or the security personnel available to do so safely. In these cases, using what are referred to as "spokespeople" becomes the best and sometimes the only feasible method for mediating a dispute.

Spokespeople are individuals selected by a group to represent their concerns and negotiate on their behalf during a mediation session. Spokespeople meet with mediators and with representatives of other groups with and sometimes without their constituencies present. In between meetings with other groups, spokespeople meet in private to report to and receive feedback from their constituencies. The advantages of using spokespeople in large group mediations include that it:

- Streamlines the discussion, saving time and energy that would be lost if everyone spoke.
- Enables disputing parties to achieve a level of intimacy and understanding that would be impossible with all parties present.
- Makes it easier for the mediators and parties to keep the discussion productive and consistent with the ground rules.
- Forces group members to communicate among themselves in order to prepare their spokespeople to represent their interests.
- Provides an audio/visual focus during the session that enables participants to hear and understand one another better.
- Reduces the time that parties miss classes or other responsibilities

because sessions are shorter and do not require the participation of all parties.

With the use of spokespeople, schools have been able to mediate large groups disputes *without ever bringing all parties together in one room.* Mediators first conduct a preliminary private session for all members of each group, during which spokespeople are selected. Next, the mediators conduct a complete mediation session—including joint and private sessions—with only the spokespeople in attendance. These individuals then return to their groups and in private, report the outcome of the sessions. The conflict is resolved if each group member's concerns were adequately addressed by their spokespeople. Sometimes the process concludes with a joint session with all parties present, a portion of which may be devoted to ceremoniously signing an agreement.

Do not use spokespeople simply because there are more parties on one side of a dispute then another. A common misconception is that there needs to be the same number of parties representing each constituency in a large group dispute. But mediation is not a tug-of-war. The mediators' job is to create an environment that is safe, affords the necessary control, and welcomes all perspectives. When this is done, the comparative number of group members becomes irrelevant because *all* parties work together to resolve their shared concerns. Besides, sometimes a group with three members exerts a far more intimidating influence in a session than a rival group with ten members. It is not unusual to mediate disputes that involve seven parties versus 15 parties, 20 versus 80, and even eight versus 26 versus 60 when more than two groups are involved.

A dramatic difference in numbers does suggest that mediators must ensure that the smaller group does not get overwhelmed by other groups. State publicly the intention to not let the relative size of the groups inhibit the process, strictly enforce ground rules, make sure each participant has an opportunity to speak, and break the time allotted to each group into manageable and roughly equal segments.

Large Groups

Selecting Spokespeople

It is imperative that spokespeople have the respect and trust of their constituencies. As a result, spokespeople are selected by the parties whenever possible. Mediators and coordinators can provide guidance to groups, suggesting the number of spokespeople to choose (usually three to five) and helping groups identify the characteristics they should look for in their representatives (a good speaker and listener, assertive, well informed about the situation, trustworthy, someone who understands different perspectives, etc.). Most times parties do a good job and choose candidates on their merits rather than on their status in the group. If there is disagreement among group members about the selection, mediators must help parties reach consensus (or risk that disgruntled participants will sabotage the process later on).

In exceptional cases, spokespeople have been selected by coordinators, mediators, and/or school staff. This occurs because the logistics or the urgency of the situation make it impossible for parties themselves to make the choice. Perhaps school vacation begins the next day, or mediators and coordinators learn that students are planning to fight at a concert two hours hence. As long as the spokespeople are a respected and representative group, this has worked out fine.

A final consideration in choosing spokespeople concerns at which stage of the process to choose them. Many factors argue for choosing spokespeople as late in the process as possible, including:

   —New parties are often identified and join the process during the early phases of a large group mediation effort. By waiting, mediators provide parties with the largest and most committed pool from which to choose spokespeople.

   —It provides the maximum number of parties with the opportunity to participate in the selection and thus support the spokespeople and the process as a whole.

   —When parties have an opportunity to observe each other during preliminary private sessions, they are more likely to select spokespeople on the basis of merit rather than popularity.

—With some exceptions, the later in the mediation effort that spokespeople are selected, the more likely that parties will select individuals who advocate collaboration rather than aggression.

Use Spokespeople Wisely

Although using spokespeople can be a tremendous aid to a large group mediation effort, the practice is not without its drawbacks. These include:

- Using spokespeople provides spokespeople only, and not their constituencies, with the opportunity to say their piece (and perhaps by the end of the session, say their "peace").
- Using spokespeople can unintentionally lock out voices of insight and reconciliation, parties who might have said to their peers: "You know, it seems like they have a point. Let's listen to them."
- Spokespeople may not accurately represent the interests of their group.
- Spokespeople may not accurately represent the substance and tenor of joint sessions back to their constituencies.

Spokespeople should therefore be used judiciously. A number of strategies can be utilized to balance the relative control that spokespeople provide with the flexibility that allows all parties to speak. Consider these:

- **Use the "open chair" method.** *All* parties attend the session, but only spokespeople are allowed to speak. A chair is placed at the front of the room for each spokesperson. In addition, mediators add one or two extra chairs per group. Anyone who is moved to speak during the sessions can occupy one of their group's open chairs and participate as a temporary spokesperson. When the individual is finished speaking, he or she returns to sit in the "audience" and leaves the chair vacant for others to follow.
- **Use spokespeople only at selected times during the process.** Spokespeople might make an initial presentation of the issues at the

start of a joint session, and then the floor can be opened to anyone with something to add. Or try the reverse of this: Begin the session by inviting anyone to speak as long as they follow the ground rules, and then later use spokespeople to negotiate the specifics of an agreement.

- **Rotate spokespeople.** Spokespeople can rotate either after a set period of time has elapsed during the session, or for each session of a multi-session mediation. This maintains the structure but gives more parties the opportunity to participate. Keep the same spokespeople, however, for sessions that deal with the same issues.

Try to remain flexible in approach and not get too attached to the format that has been created. Letting groups argue and descend into apparent confusion for a minute might help them release tension and appreciate the other side's perspective. Tolerating what seems to be an "interruption" from one party might lead to an unexpected breakthrough. Mediators create a structure for discussion only because parties have been unable to move forward without one. As soon as parties can constructively communicate on their own, mediators should get out of the way and let the parties do the work. When the size of the groups or the nature of their dispute warrants it, however, using spokespeople can be essential to conducting an effective mediation effort.

YOU CANNOT HELP
MEN PERMANENTLY BY
DOING FOR THEM
WHAT THEY COULD
AND SHOULD DO FOR
THEMSELVES.

ABRAHAM LINCOLN

It was relatively easy for the Yorkville mediators and coordinators to get parties' agreement to basic ground rules. They had some concern about the ability of the "jocks" (especially Frank) to refrain from name-calling during a joint session. Nevertheless, they felt they could move forward.

The mediation team did not feel the need to use spokespeople. Many of those attending the preliminary private session of the "worms" were not involved with the specific conflict and, after discussion with the mediators, declined to participate in the joint session. This cut the size of that group to about thirty. Eighteen

Large Groups

students were expected from the other side. Sandra and Randy
felt that because violence was unlikely, it would be best to enable
all students to benefit from direct participation in the process.
The mediators did put empty chairs at the front of each group,
however, and informed parties that they reserved the right to ask
only people sitting in those chairs to speak. In that case, they
said, anyone could come up and sit in those chairs, leaving when
they were finished speaking.

Formalize the Agenda

Mediators often take responsibility for organizing the issues in dispute and
ensuring that they are addressed by the parties. In more simple, two-party
conflicts, this is usually done informally. Referring to their notes, mediators
spontaneously guide the parties and ensure that they discuss every issue.
But in large group disputes—which may encompass a great many issues and
require multiple sessions—the agenda-setting process of necessity becomes
more formalized. Many mediators decide to create an agenda for a *series* of
mediation sessions, determining in advance which issues to discuss at each
session and in which order. In between sessions, parties implement the
agreements they have created during previous sessions.

Creating a formal agenda has these benefits. It:
- Creates realistic expectations.
- Builds positive momentum and instills a feeling of accomplishment
  in the parties.
- Helps mediators organize and control the process.
- Provides a focus for the parties.
- Helps avoid the hostility that results when issues are mixed together.
- Insures that time is used wisely.

When creating the agenda, consider the following questions:
   —Which issues are most important to the parties?
   —Which issues demand immediate attention for reasons of safety?
   —Which issues will be easiest to resolve early, thereby building parties'

confidence in the process?

—Which issues can be effectively resolved by the parties themselves through discussions outside of the mediation session?

—Which issues involve only a small percentage of the parties and would be better addressed in a separate mediation session rather than by the entire group?

The agenda that mediators create is submitted to participating groups for their approval prior to or at the beginning of each session. The agenda can then be modified according to parties' feedback. If parties are hesitant to use an agenda at all, explain that it enables mediators to maintain control (of the process) early on and can provide a path out of the confusion and animosity typical of large group disputes. Of course, mediators ultimately defer to parties' wishes, as long as this does not compromise their ability to be effective. Though not always essential, agendas can be a helpful tool in complex large group disputes.

Create an Effective Physical Environment

A final way to prepare for the complexity of large group mediation sessions concerns the physical setting, especially the seating arrangement. As in all mediations, the goal is to have the parties seated in a manner that allows for direct communication between parties as soon as this becomes appropriate, and that enables mediators to maintain control of the session (minimizing the chances that violence will occur).

Regardless of the number of disputants, it is usually preferable to have parties sit in a semi-circle facing the mediators. In addition to meeting the criteria above, this arrangement concretely demonstrates to parties that they must work together to resolve their common difficulties. It also allows mediators to view all parties without turning their heads. A common mistake is to seat groups across from one another at long tables, with the mediators at one end. This creates an adversarial tone for the proceedings and can make the work more difficult.

Some mediators go so far as to determine in advance where each party will sit in the semi-circle. Potential peacemakers might sit on the inside of the semi-circle next to members of the other group, while volatile "hotheads" are separated and seated towards the outside, shielded by members of their own group. This author is aware of a variety of sometimes contradictory seating approaches. Where one says the exit should be behind the mediators, another suggests that the exit should be behind the parties (with physically imposing support people in front of the door). Needless to say, consider the parties involved and if it appears beneficial, ask them to sit in a location that seems most appropriate.

Sitting parties in a semi-circle might not be adequate when tensions and the potential for violence are high, however. In these cases, a physical barrier—most commonly tables—can be placed between groups to discourage physical confrontations. Sitting behind the tables provides parties with a sense of safety that would be absent were there only open space between groups. Tables also create a business-like, "let's get to work" tone.

When the total number of parties is under 20, it is usually possible to have parties sit at tables in a *single* semi-circle facing the mediators. When the number of parties is greater than this, set up chairs in large, concentric semi-circles. A central aisle (empty or with tables as barrier) and a couple of tables at the front of each group can be used to mark space. One excellent place to hold large group mediation sessions is a music rehearsal area that has graduated levels rising towards the rear and arranged in a semi-circle. Chairs are placed on the risers, tables are situated at the bottom for spokespeople, parties can all see each other easily, and the initial focus is on the mediators at front.

During early joint sessions, it is inevitable that parties will sit with members of their own group. As hostilities decrease and parties come to trust one another, groups may intermingle and a party from one side will seat him/herself next to a party from the other. This is heartening and indicative

Large Groups

of the progress of the mediation. During long sessions or over the course of a series of sessions, consider changing the seating arrangement to encourage dialogue and the dissolution of barriers between groups. Putting chairs in a full circle rather than a semi-circle, removing tables and other obstructions, meeting in more relaxed settings, if appropriately timed, will all help move the process forward.

Apart from the seating arrangement, other strategies for creating an effective setting in which to mediate large groups disputes include:

- Use flip charts or a chalkboard to write down important information during the session.
- Make a seating chart as an aid to learn parties' names. Mediators ask participants to sit in the same place for the first few sessions, draw a diagram of the seats, and write parties' names according to where they sit. With so many things to do at once in large group mediations, it is helpful to have at least one concern mapped out ahead of time.
- Create name "tents" that sit on the tables in front of spokespeople.
- Use comfortable chairs (from the school committee room?) rather than hard metal ones.
- Place pitchers of ice-water and cups on the tables.
- Provide refreshments during breaks.
- Give a pad of paper and a pencil to each party.

These and similar actions establish a dignified tone that communicates to parties that they are important and respected. And when parties feel respected, they are more likely to respect the mediators, the process, and each other. This sort of intervention is especially helpful with young people who are chronically alienated from school and from adults. Remember that showing respect for parties during the process doesn't mean mediators condone their actions.

In Yorkville, the coordinator arranged the chairs in a semi-circle. There were too many parties to sit in one circle, so they sat in a number of concentric circles. Ethan and Gomez were asked in advance to sit on the front edge of their groups. The rest sat wherever they wanted on their group's side. Even though the student supporters had placed chairs exactly as the mediators requested, Nate, Frank and a few other students immediately moved their chairs to the back corner of the room. The mediators delivered their opening remarks, then requested that these students move forward into their group. They begrudgingly complied. Plastic containers of water and soda were placed on a table near each group. Name tags were created in advance for parties to wear, but most students were unwilling to wear them.

Hours and maybe days may have passed since the large group dispute was first referred. The extensive preparatory work outlined above, work that will serve the process well, has been completed. Finally, the time may be right to bring groups together and begin the phase that is the heart of the mediation process: Joint Sessions.

Phase III: Joint Sessions and Beyond

"Joint sessions" refer to the sessions in which the groups in conflict, or their spokespeople, meet together and negotiate face-to-face with the assistance of the mediators. Once the first joint session of a large group mediation is conducted, the process follows much the same format as interpersonal mediation sessions. The fundamental structure, intervention techniques, and strategies are the same. Private sessions (as opposed to preliminary private sessions discussed above) may occur between joint sessions, or during breaks in the middle of a joint session. When facilitating joint sessions involving large groups, mediators emphasize certain aspects of the process and utilize others in unique ways. A number of suggestions are presented below:

Schedule adequate time for the session

Although each case is different, mediators usually schedule at least three hours for the initial joint session. Parties may need to vent the strong emotions associated with the conflict first, before they can more calmly address the issues in dispute. Mediating without enough time is not only inadvisable, it can be dangerous to send emotionally distressed parties back into the school community prematurely. It is usually preferable to not begin a joint session at all than to begin without adequate time.

> *The mediators scheduled the initial joint session for three and one half hours, with a fifteen minute break in the middle. The session actually lasted four hours and twenty minutes.*

Emphasize the ground rules for participation

Acknowledge to parties that although they might be uncomfortable at the outset, these feelings usually fade as the session progresses. A formal agreement to participate can help here. If the parties break the ground rules (for instance, by threatening one another) mediators need to swiftly and respectfully enforce them. Neglecting to do so can cause the process to break down and force mediators to conduct themselves like disciplinarians.

> *The Yorkville mediators posted a copy of the ground rules on the wall behind them, and they reviewed each rule before they began. At one point during the joint session, Jolie and two other girls started taunting Christine. When the latter responded in kind, Jolie stood up and challenged her to fight. Randy rose in response and calmly asked Jolie to sit down. After a long pause, he reviewed the ground rules and asked the girls if they could continue in a productive manner. They said they could. Randy asked the girls to move their seats to the outside edge of their groups for now, and they both complied.*

Clarify expectations

During the first joint session, present an overview of the plan for the entire process: how many sessions have been scheduled; the days, times and locations for those sessions; tentative agendas for each session, etc. At the start of each subsequent session, mediators outline the process they expect to follow, including the proposed agenda and goals, the process that will be used for speaking, the length of the session, and the expected use of private sessions. Make sure that parties understand, support and to the extent possible, co-create this plan.

> *Sandra, Randy and their team did not feel the need to set a formal agenda for the first joint session. The parties' concerns as they understood them appeared relatively narrow and did not warrant limiting the scope of the students' discussion so early.*

Allow each group to completely explain their version of events

It seems obvious, but some mediators neglect this because *they* have already learned about the conflict during preliminary private sessions. The sheer number of parties, the gravity and possible urgency of the situation, and the fact that hearing the complete, often convoluted story might be very time consuming can also be daunting to mediators. Yet hearing the other side's "story" is extremely valuable and potentially transformative for parties. In most cases, parties in their first joint session have never heard the complete version of events as told by the other group. Be sure to enable each group (or their spokespeople) to tell their complete story without interruption. If the length of the presentations becomes problematic, limit the amount of time that each group has to present their perspective.

> *All parties were hesitant to speak at the start of the joint session. After a pause, Christine outlined her concerns. She concluded by saying that she just wanted to be left alone to live her own life. A number of other "worms" followed. Gomez said he didn't like the prejudice he was seeing, and he hoped that everyone would work to end the conflict and "get back to just being normal students in school." Billie did not say a word during the initial presentation, even after the mediators encouraged him to speak. The "jocks" appeared to be listening for the most part, although the mediators (and one time Roy Johnson) had to ask them to*

stop snickering to one another. When no additional "worms" wanted to speak, Sandra summarized their concerns and asked the "jocks" to explain their perspective.

Frank began by explaining why he thought the races should be kept separate. This engendered shouts of protest from some of the "worms." Ethan, a fellow "jock," even said, "Frank, will you shut up!" Randy had to ask them all to stop interrupting, and then he requested that Frank continue, encouraging him to focus on the task at hand. Frank replied: "Well that is between Nate and his sister."

Nate said that he didn't have much to say, just that "I don't like the kid" (referring to Billie). He responded to the mediators' questions with clipped answers. When they got an opportunity to speak, Matthew mentioned the graffiti on his house and Tony said he wanted to find out about his windshield. Some other "jocks" implied that the "worms" were using the race issue to get them in trouble. By the time Sandra summarized the concerns of the "jocks," one hour and twenty minutes of the session had elapsed.

The mediators then had the groups speak directly to one another. Although the discussion was passionate and at times seemingly chaotic, it appeared that progress was being made. One of the "worms" said he was sorry about the graffiti on Matthew's house, but added that he hadn't done it and he didn't think any of the kids in the room had. Gomez and Ethan announced that there was no longer a problem between them. Nate and Billie remained quiet, however.

Hold private sessions and breaks when needed

Even though the group may be large and logistics may be more difficult, do not hesitate to take private sessions or breaks. Mediators do this to:

- Explore issues too volatile or sensitive to discuss in a public session.
- Allow spokespeople time to meet with their constituents to discuss

the proceedings.*

- Provide mediators time to collect their thoughts, speak to each other in private, and strategize.
- Provide parties with an opportunity to broach issues that they are too uncomfortable to mention during joint sessions.
- Calm parties down or allow them time to stretch and relax.
- Provide a graceful way to excuse parties who are no longer needed at the session.
- Enable mediators to call in various combinations of parties from opposing "sides." Mediators use this strategy to balance the power (if there are many more parties on one side than on the other), to discuss issues relevant only to particular parties, and to explore alliances across the boundaries of the dispute. This last reason is especially noteworthy. Sometimes parties who act like aggressive adversaries in the joint session will resolve their differences surprisingly easily when they speak directly in private. They then become a conciliatory force within their groups. Two cautions: Make sure mediators inform parties at the start of the session that they might speak to them in strange combinations, and be cognizant of the pressure that parties will feel from friends and allies who are not in the room.

Sandra and Randy called for a number of private sessions. The first break was necessitated by inflammatory comments from Frank, comments which upset the "worms" and led to threats back and forth. The mediators decided to take a break and collect themselves. The "worms" were asked to leave the room accompanied by Roy Johnson, the "jocks" stayed put with Joy Chin, and the mediators went into an anteroom to speak. Concerned about Billie's silence, the mediators asked Roy to pull Billie aside and make sure he was comfortable with the process so far. Billie told Roy that he was.

---

* It is preferable if these meetings occur in separate rooms, but they can be held in the corners of a large room so long as groups won't hear one another.

After the break, the mediators called Frank and Nate in alone to listen to their concerns, continue to win their trust, and clarify whether they wanted to proceed with mediation. They both expressed a desire to continue: Nate apparently genuinely, but Frank with a wry grin that left the mediators uncertain.

A second private session was composed of basketball players from both groups. Garfield and a couple of other "worms" played basketball along with Tony, and comments during the joint session indicated to Sandra that it would be helpful to have them all meet privately. This turned out to be the case when Garfield, Tony and the others agreed that the situation was "stupid" and said they wanted to accept one another regardless of what "group you are a part of."

Actively highlight the positive

Think of a balloon—from even a tiny pinprick, it deflates very quickly. The same is true of many large group conflicts. Once parties begin to resolve the tensions that have created them, their energy inevitably and often rapidly dissipates. One way mediators "prick the balloon" is by highlighting the positive—discussing the progress that has been made and the misunderstandings that have been clarified.

Groups will sometimes resist this progress and drown out the growing number among them who recognize the legitimacy of their adversaries' concerns. Every time one party says something conciliatory, a member of their own group will exclaim: "But wait, remember when they did such and such to us!" Counter this tendency by asking parties who are ready to work together to demonstrate their willingness *concretely*: perhaps by standing together in a certain section of the room, perhaps by shaking the hand of someone from another group. When this type of intervention is appropriately timed, a great deal of tension will evaporate in an instant.

Such a turning point does not mean that the conflict is resolved. Issues remain to be discussed, and discrete interpersonal conflicts may need to be mediated separately. But the intergroup hostility that tends to escalate tensions will largely dissipate, making it easier to focus on other issues at hand.

> *Gomez and Ethan's reconciliation was one example of progress that the mediators used to dissolve the large group tensions. Other factors that were discovered during the joint session and highlighted later by the mediators were that:*
> - *Apparently none of the "worm" participants wrote the graffiti on the side of Matthew's house.*
> - *Many of the "jocks" did not like Frank and Nate's aggressive racism and supported the "worms" in this regard.*
> - *All parties, especially those on the basketball team, wanted to end the conflict between the groups.*
> - *Most parties agreed that the root of the conflict was a family problem in the Jones household.*

Keep spirits up

Things rarely proceed as planned in large group mediations. Progress comes in fits and starts, and sometimes things get worse before they get better. An important party might not agree to participate or not show up, or a session might end with few visible gains and an even greater level of open hostility between parties than prior to mediation. Mediators, coordinators and support staff should arrange to meet before and after every session in order to support and encourage one another. It is essential to maintain a positive attitude and be prepared for setbacks: the parties and the process depend upon this.

This is not to say that mediators need be Pollyannas. There are occasions when a mediator can push the process forward by appropriately expressing his or her honest concern or frustration about a situation. As always, timing and great sensitivity are key here.

> *The only serious setback during the Yorkville case was that Frank and a friend got up and left during the second joint ses-*

WHEN YOU GET INTO A TIGHT PLACE AND EVERYTHING GOES AGAINST YOU, TILL IT SEEMS AS THOUGH YOU COULD NOT HANG ON A MINUTE LONGER, NEVER GIVE UP THEN, FOR THAT IS JUST THE PLACE AND TIME THAT THE TIDE WILL TURN.

HARRIET BEECHER STOWE

Large Groups

sion. Mr. Melhoon followed after them and tried to convince them to return, but they were unwilling to do so. Although this put a temporary damper on the commitment of the "jock" group, in the long run it was a positive development. The remaining "jocks" were more amenable to reconciliation with the "worms," and within fifty minutes of Frank's departure, the parties had created a sound agreement.

Ensure that agreements are realistic

School-based mediators typically help parties create written agreements at the conclusion of the process. Although this holds true for large group conflicts as well, the size and complexity of these disputes means that many factors can de-stabilize any agreement that is reached. Parties not involved in the session (even individuals not attending the school) can act as instigators; the negative impact of peer pressure is magnified; and minor "sparks" involving only a few parties can re-ignite the conflict between entire groups. It is therefore especially important to help parties create agreements that are realistic given their circumstances.

Usually this leads mediators to limit agreements in some way. Agreements can be time-limited (parties agree to do things until the next session, for one week, during the school day), space-limited (parties agree to refrain from doing things on school grounds or when in each other's neighborhoods), and limited in their scope. Interim agreements can be created and then evaluated in subsequent meetings.

Mediators should also discuss with parties how they will handle potentially de-stabilizing factors. What will happen if they hear a rumor? How will they inform others about what happened in the mediation session? If there is a problem, can they approach parties directly or should they come to the mediation office first? These and related questions should be considered.

The Yorkville mediators wisely helped the students create specific points of agreement to ensure their success (see page 200 for the

(see page 200 for the

Large Groups

list). The parties arranged for a one-week trial period for the agreement, scheduled a follow-up meeting, and directly addressed the potential problem of rumors. Although it was not included in the agreement, all parties also agreed to tell others that the situation was resolved. Mr. Melhoon put out soda, donuts and fruit at the conclusion of the session, and many parties lingered in the room, eating the refreshments and talking with each other informally.

The completion of the third phase of large group mediation, Joint Sessions, marks the end of the mediation proper. Even if reconciliation or agreement between parties *does not* result, chances are good that the effort will have de-escalated the conflict in important ways. Then it is time to move on to the final phase of large group mediating: Follow-up.

Phase IV: Follow-up

Just as the "birth" of an agreement requires extra care in large group mediations, a more intensive approach to follow-up is also necessary. Even when no agreement is reached, coordinators and/or mediators will likely need to follow-up with parties. Here are some suggestions:

Ensure that interpersonal disputes are resolved

As previously discussed, most large group disputes contain a collection of two-party disputes. Just as resolving the interpersonal disputes does not in and of itself end the group conflict, so too resolving the group dispute may leave discrete interpersonal conflicts intact. Parties may even learn information during joint sessions that serves to intensify their antipathy towards a particular individual. These parties may not be willing or able to publicly voice their new concerns during the mediation process (waiting instead until the next day in the halls).

Mediators and coordinators should seek out parties who are still in conflict at the conclusion of the group mediation and offer to help. The difficulty of speaking with individual parties amidst the controlled chaos of the largest group disputes usually necessitates that mediators approach parties after the session.

After concluding the large group mediation process, Sandra, Randy and their support team identified three interpersonal disputes that appeared to require further attention. One involved Danielle, the middle school student who allegedly broke Tony's windshield. Both parties were interested, and the following week Mr. Melhoon scheduled a mediation session with two student mediators. Private sessions proved key in this mediation; only in private did Danielle admit to breaking the windshield "by accident." She said she felt badly about this. In his private session, Tony explained that he wanted only an apology from Danielle because his parents' insurance had paid for the windshield. The mediators were able to facilitate the sharing of this information in a subsequent joint session, and both Tony and Danielle left the session relieved and ready to move on.

The second, more challenging session involved Christine and her brother, Nate. Towards the end of the large group joint session, Christine had made an impassioned plea to her brother to sit down and talk, to which he hesitantly agreed. Mr. Melhoon scheduled a session for them the next week. (He had asked them whether they wanted their mother present, but both did not.) Mr. Melhoon co-mediated the case along with a student mediator with whom Nate felt comfortable. The session was very poignant, with some small progress in communication and Nate agreeing to "let Christine live her own life." At Christine's request, the mediators also asked the school adjustment counselor to set up an appointment for her.

The third potential mediation session involved Billie and Nate, but when Mr. Melhoon approached Billie the next day, he refused to mediate privately with Nate. Billie said that since they did not see each other in school very much, he thought it would be best to have nothing to do with Nate from now on. (The two had informally agreed to leave each other alone during the large group session.) Mr. Melhoon—Sandra Joyce was no longer directly involved in the process—was disappointed, and stressed to Billie that as long as he was dating Christine, he and Nate would likely have contact. But there was no convincing Billie.

Inform administrators

Just as mediators need to gain administrative support on the front end of a large group mediation, it is usually advisable for them to meet with administrators after the mediation process has concluded. The limits of confidentiality usually require that mediators and coordinators say no more than whether the conflict is resolved and thank administrators for their willingness to support the process. The meeting does provide an opportunity to inform administrators about actions they can take to support the implementation of an agreement, actions that may have been requested by the parties. Perhaps a group prefers not to be referred to by a certain name, or parties want administrators' misconception about what motivated the conflict corrected. It is even possible that parties want administrators to consider modifying school policies that they feel contributed to the mistrust between them (forcing groups to sit in specific areas of the cafeteria, for instance). Meeting with administrators solidifies support for future mediation efforts, helps to ensure the success of resolutions that have been reached, and alerts them when a conflict demands their continued attention.

Ms. Aramian was relieved to learn from Mr. Melhoon on Friday afternoon that the conflict appeared to be resolved. The parties had asked Mr. Melhoon to inform her that they were writing a letter of apology to Matthew's parents. Mr. Melhoon also conveyed, at the request of the "worms," that some students were concerned about the prejudicial behavior of a few staff members. Ms. Aramian asked if these students would like to meet with her directly. Mr. Melhoon said he would convey her invitation to them.

Be sensitive to the dispute's impact upon the rest of the school

The entire school community is sometimes aware of large group disputes. These conflicts often raise issues that are of great concern to others in the school, issues such as racism, violence and school safety. It therefore may be important for coordinators and mediators to help individuals who were not party to the conflict come to terms with its impact. This usually takes the form of discussion groups, facilitated by coordinators, mediators and skilled teachers, and conducted for groups of administrators, staff and students. If all goes well, mediating large group disputes can lead to school-wide improvements as well as generate positive publicity for a peer mediation program.

After the mediation process was complete, a core group of students from both sides of the dispute—Garfield, Christine, and Ethan among them—began to meet occasionally to explore their differences. Their eventual goal was to reach out to all students with a message of appreciation of diversity. The group and their volunteer faculty advisors were also exploring the possibility of organizing a special training on diversity for staff and students.

Intensify follow-up contact

Plan regular, semi-formal follow-up meetings to assess the effectiveness of the agreement and to make necessary modifications. When possible, include these meetings as part of the written agreement ("All parties agree to come to a meeting on March 3rd to discuss how things are going"). Also check in with parties separately, arranging to meet with them individually or in small groups. Some programs distribute a follow-up questionnaire to all parties a few days to two weeks after the session. An especially promising follow-up practice involves providing conflict resolution and communication skills training to interested parties. Coordinators, mediators, and other support people can do this work. Vigilance in the weeks after the agreement is created ensures that minor difficulties are resolved expediently and do not jeopardize the larger peace.

> *Mr. Melhoon and his co-coordinators' follow-up efforts were multifaceted. The centerpiece was informal meetings with most of the parties during the weeks following the session. Mr. Melhoon even had a long meeting with Frank in private, and because the latter spoke a little about his difficulties at home, Mr. Melhoon felt that Frank had taken a small step towards trusting him.*

> *Christine came to the office one day and claimed that Jolie was threatening to fight her. This led to a mediation session between the two which Mr. Melhoon himself conducted on the spot. During the session, Jolie admitted that she was upset that Christine was saying derogatory comments about her to Nate and to their mother. In the end, although they were far from friends, the two agreed to stop instigating trouble with one another.*

> *Garfield sought out Mr. Melhoon a week after the mediation session for assistance with a teacher who he felt was saying racist remarks in front of class. They spent a long time talking, and in the end decided together that the best course of action was for Garfield to approach the teacher in private and express his concerns. Mr. Melhoon coached Garfield extensively regarding expressing himself in a way that the teacher could understand.*

> *Mr. Melhoon also maintained contact with parties by letter. The Monday after the joint session, he sent the following letter to all parties:*

>> *To all students who participated in the mediation session on Friday—*
>> *Thank you for your cooperation and patience. The process of becoming aware and showing respect for others has taken a giant step forward. We hope to offer programs in the near future that will support our commitment to respect others.*

I hope you will show your parents the agreement you created. In addition, please invite them to a follow-up meeting (for parents only) to be held next Monday at 7:00 p.m. in the conference room. If they are unable to attend and would like to speak with the principal, counselor, or me about these matters, they can reach us at school at 535-2900.

The mediators will return on Friday, March 25 to meet with all of us and review how things are going. Please meet in room 342 at 11:00.

I will close by listing the seven items in your agreement. If any problems arise, please contact Ms. Chin, Mr. Johnson, or me immediately.

1. *We all agree that the fight between the two groups is over.*

2. *We all agree to respect each other and not put other people down because of their race, religion, class, or clique.*

3. *For the next week, if we hear a rumor we will either speak to the person directly (if we can do so without fighting), or we will go talk to Mr. Melhoon or Mr. Johnson and get their help.*

4. *We agree that if individual conflicts do exist, we will not blow them up into group conflicts.*

5. *The "worms" agree to write a letter to Matthew's parents saying that although they did not write the graffiti on their house, they are very sorry that it happened. They will mail the letter by next Tuesday.*

6. *Everyone agrees to make an effort to keep the peace and make Yorkville High School a better place.*

7. *We will all meet again in one week on Friday, March 25th at 11:00 in room 342 to see how things are going.*

Large Group Mediation: Preparation, Skill, Flexibility

This chapter suggests an ideal process for mediating large group disputes. A great deal of time and effort is required, especially in the form of preparation, but this investment is rewarded with effective mediation sessions that help parties resolve complex disputes. Use this chapter as a guide when designing a process for large group mediations.

Every large group mediation need not incorporate every suggestion offered in this chapter, however. A disagreement involving groups of friends concerning rumors about boyfriends requires a different response than a cafeteria brawl between a school's white and Hispanic populations. Sometimes schools have neither the time nor the resources to do a great deal of preparation before mediating a large group dispute. The situation may be urgent, or the mediators may have only a few days in their schedule to devote to the case. In some instances, groups of disputing students have been ushered into a joint session with little advance warning and only two hours to mediate, and there has still been significant, albeit limited, progress. Though far from the ideal, these impromptu large group mediation efforts can work. Mediators should gauge what is required for each case.

One final point is essential to bear in mind. Despite the best efforts of coordinators and mediators, mediating large group disputes is always a controlled improvisation. Parties may stand up and wander about, rules are upheld and broken and upheld again, people argue and shout, new parties show up and old ones disappear. Not only is this impossible to prevent, the disorder sometimes serves a purpose by uncovering issues and getting parties emotionally invested. The best mediators—and it is essential to have the best mediators for these disputes—discard their well-made plans spontaneously at the prospect of something that might work better. The crucial work of mediating large group disputes, like all mediating, takes place in the moment.

Large Groups

Checklist
CHAPTER 8: MEDIATING LARGE GROUP DISPUTES

GARNERING SUPPORT FOR MEDIATION

✓ Gain administrative support (158)

✓ Identify skilled mediators (159)

✓ Arrange for school staff and community members to provide: (160)
- Logistical support
- Support for parties
- Support for mediators
- Follow-up support
- Interpretation

ASSESSMENT, PREPARATION, AND PRELIMINARY PRIVATE SESSIONS

✓ Decide whether to initially meet with groups in preliminary private sessions or in a joint session (164)

✓ Identify, gather, and interview the parties (167)

✓ Determine the extent to which parties' parents will be involved (169)

✓ Determine whether initial meetings will be group intake interviews, preliminary private sessions, or both (171)

✓ Identify and attend to discrete interpersonal disputes as early in the process as possible (176)

✓ Formalize the agreement to participate and include generic as well as conflict-specific points of agreement (180)

✓ Control who will speak using ground rules (182)

✓ Use spokespeople when necessary: (184)
- Help groups select their own spokespeople *as late in the process as appropriate*
- Remain flexible and stop using spokespeople as soon as parties can communicate constructively without them

✓ Formalize the agenda (189)

✓ Create an effective physical environment: (190)
- Identify a safe site for mediation
- Use a semicircular seating arrangement
- Use tables as barriers
- Assign seats for specific parties when necessary

- Create a dignified tone by using flip charts or a chalkboard, creating name "tents," and providing paper, pencils and refreshments

JOINT SESSIONS

✓ Schedule adequate time for joint sessions (194)

✓ Emphasize the ground rules for participation (194)

✓ Clarify expectations at the start by presenting an overview of the entire process (194)

✓ Allow each group to completely explain their version of events (195)

✓ Hold private sessions and breaks when necessary (196)

✓ Actively highlight the positive (198)

✓ Keep spirits up (199)

✓ Ensure that agreements are realistic (200)

FOLLOW-UP

✓ Ensure that discrete interpersonal disputes are resolved (201)

✓ Inform administrators about the status of the mediation effort and any actions they can take to support the process (203)

✓ Be sensitive to the dispute's impact upon the rest of the school (204)

✓ Intensify follow-up contact (204)

Large Groups

MEDIATING
CONFLICTS
INVOLVING
YOUTH GANGS

Youth gangs have existed in large North American cities for genera-
tions. But over the last ten years, gangs have relocated or formed in
smaller cities and towns that had never seen gang activity before.
By the mid 1990's, ever increasing numbers of schools have had to contend
with their students joining gangs as well as with members of rival gangs
interacting on school grounds.

Read Chapter Eight for
the fundamentals of medi-
ating conflicts involving
large groups.

The reasons behind the growth of youth gangs are complex: broken families, dim economic prospects for young people, racism, poverty—all forces in
contemporary society that child advocates bemoan. A recent report from the
United States Department of Justice states that "...the lack of social opportunities available to a population and the degree of social disorganization present in a community largely account for its youth gang problem."[30]
Tragically, in some of the most troubled communities, the problems associated with gangs—horrible violence, drug use, dropping out of school—are epi-
demic. Sometimes students' older siblings and even parents have been
members of a gang. And as some of the few individuals in their neighborhoods who appear to have "made it," gang members can become role models
for young people.

Students join gangs to satisfy *normal* physical and psychological needs, needs
that their peers meet through socially acceptable affiliations with family,

school, and religious institutions (and to a lesser extent with sports teams, clubs, musical groups, and after-school jobs). Young people who successfully meet their needs through these "normal" channels generally do not become involved in gangs. But for students who are unable to satisfy their basic needs through *any* channel, gangs can provide what they lack: safety and security, companionship, a common purpose, things to do, and a sense of family, duty, power, and even love. It is illustrative to note that some gang members take pride in the recognition that comes with their outlaw status, showing each other newspaper clippings that recount their crimes and regarding criminal records as badges of honor.

IF WE COULD READ
THE SECRET HISTORY
OF OUR ENEMIES, WE
SHOULD FIND IN EACH
MAN'S LIFE SORROW
AND SUFFERING
ENOUGH TO DISARM
ALL HOSTILITY.

HENRY WADSWORTH
LONGFELLOW

Gang-related conflicts at school are likely to be some of the most difficult cases school-based mediators will face. This is because these conflicts (whether between gang members and non-gang members, within a single gang, or between rival gangs) serve a deep psychological function for gang members. Outside enemies create a sense of purpose and loyalty within gangs, defining for members who they are and why they exist. In gangs that have been in existence for decades, inter-gang rivalries are passed on and maintained by members who don't even know the origins of the tension.

Gangs

Mediation has been employed successfully to contain and even resolve gang tensions in schools across North America. This application of the mediation process is in its infancy, however, and school-based mediators appear to have mediated relatively few gang-related conflicts. Although those who work at community-based gang intervention and prevention report that they "mediate," in most instances these individuals have no formal mediation training and do not apply the process typical of school-based mediators.[*] Nevertheless, the clear strengths of the mediation process and the success reported to date warrant further application and exploration.

---

[*] This is not meant to denigrate the extremely important work done by gang specialists, only to clarify that their experiences are not directly applicable to school-based mediators.

What Kind of Gang?

When a youth gang conflict is referred to mediation, it is important to clarify what the referral source means by "gang." Significantly, the "experts" themselves disagree about what constitutes a gang. Relatively few young people fit the stereotypical profile of gang members promulgated by the media: kids with guns selling drugs for profit. Though academics have developed a number of contrasting typologies, the following five criteria have been widely used in research to describe youth gangs:

1. A formal organizational structure
2. Identifiable leadership
3. Identification with a territory
4. Members who interact regularly
5. Engagement in anti-social or violent behavior[31]

Many so-called "social gangs" primarily offer affiliation and camaraderie, and meet some combination of the above criteria excepting the last. The personal relationships among members is their raison d'être, and their main function is social, not economic. These groups range from friends who spend time together but who have no formal organization, to highly organized groups who have initiation rituals, traditions, and their own manners of speech and dress. Social gang members are easier to recognize because they often take pride in identifying themselves with their gang. Members of these gangs may commit interpersonal violence and petty crimes, but usually only to defend their neighborhood turf, their ethnic/racial heritage, or their personal and collective honor.

Youth gangs organized for economic more than for social purposes have been called "corporate gangs" or "drug gangs." These highly structured criminal conspiracies deal drugs or engage in other serious crimes. Members of corporate gangs would not draw attention to themselves by wearing special clothes. They are disciplined and uphold a code of silence.

Gangs

In many communities in North America, it is important to consider whether students involved in alleged "gang" disputes are part of gangs at all. The latter half of the 1980's into the 1990's saw the rise in popularity of urban, primarily African-American, culture among all young people.* One example: Rap music, originally a black, urban musical form, has been one of the fastest growing types of music in the United States during the 1990's. Along with this new youth culture has come a language and an attitude among young people that is foreign to many adults. In some instances, the difference between youth and adult culture has led to misunderstandings regarding gangs and their involvement in disputes.

The word "posse" is illustrative. First used by urban gang members to describe themselves, as in the "D Street Posse," "posse" is currently used by some students to refer to any group that spends time together. People who live in the same neighborhood, have a common interest, or are part of the same clique of friends might be referred to as part of the same "posse." Language once associated with gangs is thus now part of the everyday lexicon of young people. When such language is delivered with the anger and bravado characteristic of interpersonal conflict ("I'm going to get my boys on you!"), it can appear to adults that students are referring to real gangs when they are simply referring to their friends. Many referrals of "gang" disputes may not involve real gangs at all.

This last caution should not minimize the serious problems associated with youth gangs. Ask students in many urban schools if they know of young people who died or were seriously injured from gang violence, and far too many will raise their hands. It is only meant to underscore the need to "do your homework" and ascertain the nature of the groups involved. Gang activity is variable. What is harmless in one community could be life-threatening in another. A mediation coordinator should do this kind of pre-

---

* This should not imply that gangs are solely a product of African-American culture, or that most gang members are black. Young people of all races and ethnic backgrounds become involved in gangs.

liminary assessment as a matter of course in all large group disputes. Only then can the process move forward in an appropriate manner.

As far as this author can establish, to date school-based mediators have primarily intervened in disputes involving informal groups or social gangs, and usually those that are not highly organized. The majority of these disputes have concerned typical student issues: rumors, wounded pride, teasing and harassment, boyfriend/girlfriend difficulties, and turf problems. Mediation has prevented conflicts before they start as well as calmed tensions that otherwise would have led to violence and injury. One school, anticipating trouble between rival gangs, conducted a mediation session at the beginning of the school year. The session was conducted by former gang members who had been trained as mediators. At its conclusion, parties agreed to make the school grounds off limits for any expression of the tension between them. They also agreed to use the mediation process when conflicts did arise.

EVEN PORCUPINES HAVE A SOFT BELLY.

NATIVE AMERICAN SAYING

Corporate gangs generally do not cause trouble within schools; their members are unlikely to attend school at all. When corporate gang activity is discovered in a school, it is a matter for law enforcement and only secondarily for mediation. Of course, the proper authorities should always be notified whenever illegal or dangerous activities are taking place on school grounds, regardless of what type of gang is involved.

Signs of Gang Presence

How does one know whether gangs are operating in a school? If school-based mediators are savvy or have developed trusting relationships with students, chances are good that they know already. Students will tell them, and mediators may have personal relationships with gang members. But in schools where gangs are a new problem, adults as well as many students may not be aware of gangs' presence. Experienced school mediators counsel the importance of pro-actively determining whether gangs exist in a school; otherwise, their activity may not surface until after conflicts that involve a

Gangs

great deal of interpersonal animosity have erupted.* Look for the following signs of gang presence and inter-gang tensions in school:

—**Gang related dress, graffiti, or hand signals.** Although gang behavior is specific to time and place, some broad generalizations are possible. One sign of gang activity involves students wearing specific articles of clothing or clothing with specific colors. Gang members create graffiti with their collective name or their own personal "tag" or nickname, graffiti which might be found on desks and books, in bathrooms, and on outside walls and sidewalks. Many gangs use hand gestures which announce gang affiliation.

—**Gang recruitment at school.** When gangs are forming or preparing to fight, they try to recruit new members. Gang-affiliated students may intimidate their peers into becoming members, and the latter may complain that they are being pressured to join a gang. There may be initiation rituals happening on or near school grounds. One such ritual reported by mediators at the New Mexico Center for Dispute Resolution, "ranking in," involves gang members beating up prospective members to see how tough they are. If the young person can take the beating, they are allowed to join the gang. If they can't, they "rank out" and are pummeled even harder.

—**An increase and/or a pattern of conflict between distinct group of students.** This seems so obvious as to not be worth mentioning, but often it is overlooked by educators unaware of gang activity. Although the conflicts may concern minor and everyday student issues, gangs may still be involved.

—**Weapons.** The presence or increase in the number of weapons confiscated on school property is another indication of gang tension. The weapons might be objects not first associated with fighting such as sticks, baseball bats, or silverware. They can be found in students'

* In their article "Youth Gangs Aren't Just A Big City Problem Anymore" (The Executive Educator, July 1990), Anthony Moriarty and Thomas W. Fleming state that "the biggest victory a gang member can score in a school is to walk by the principal flaunting gang colors—and walk away unscathed" (p. 15).

possession or hidden in bushes or alleys near school property.

—**Presence of outsiders.** The presence or increase of outsiders loiter-
ing near the school, especially at the start and finish of the school
day, is a sign that gang tensions might be escalating. Students
invite other gang members to school for protection and support
should a fight occur.

Suggestions for Mediating Gang Disputes

The actual process for mediating conflicts between gangs is similar to the
process used to mediate any large group dispute. All of the strategies coordinators and mediators employ to manage the complexity of large group disputes, strategies discussed in depth in Chapter 8, are relevant here. Read
that chapter for the basics. Special considerations that apply to gang mediations include:

• **Work closely with community-based individuals and agencies.** As one
gang intervention specialist put it: "Everything that happens in the
neighborhood, happens in school." One community that had six rival
gangs found that each level of their six-story high school was "controlled"
by a different gang. When a fight or other dramatic gang-related incident occurs in the neighborhood, educators feel the effects in their classrooms the next day.

It is important that school-based mediators collaborate with individuals
and agencies who either work with gang-involved youth, or who gang
members respect and regard as community leaders. The basic advantages
of including support people in large group mediation sessions are discussed in Chapter 8. As far as gang disputes are concerned, support
people can:
  —help mediators learn about the gangs
  —enable mediators to build trust with gang members by serving as a
      bridge between school culture and gang culture
  —arrange preliminary meetings with gang members, something which

Gangs

in and of itself can be a difficult task

—speak with gang members who don't attend school and request that they respect any agreement that student gang members create

—connect gang members with on-going programs and services

—help with follow-up and support of an agreement

—depending on their skills, serve as mediators or mediation assistants

Mediation coordinators also report that gang-affiliated students sometimes come to them for assistance when they no longer want to be involved in gangs. Coordinators can refer these students to community-based gang specialists who can help with the difficult and potentially dangerous task of extricating themselves from gang life.

- **Learn about gangs in the area.** Each gang has its own norms, expectations of members, focus, and level of organization. Differences in the "culture" of gangs composed of members of the same race or ethnic background, for instance, have been widely documented. There is also a wide range in the degree to which gangs are involved with illegal activities. The more that mediators know about a particular gang, the easier it will be to win their trust and work effectively with them.

- **Choose mediators wisely.** Mediating always involves some risk, but legal liability and the potential for violence increases in gang-related disputes. Student mediators have been used to mediate disputes between two individual gang members. But most schools employ adult mediators for conflicts that involve many gang members. The peer mediation coordinator or community mediators who are familiar with gangs and have gang members' respect (gang workers, religious leaders, etc.) are worthy candidates. Ex-gang members and even active gang members themselves—if they have been trained as mediators and if they will be perceived as neutral by all parties—can also be very effective mediators. Although some educators express concern that using gang members to mediate "rewards" them for their gang status, the opportunity to enable gang-affiliated students to make a positive contribution to school and community makes this a risk many coordinators are willing to take. One coordinator says: "Gang members already have status among their peers; serving as a mediator helps them use their status in a positive way."

- **Emphasize the trust building process.** Gangs devote a good deal of their energy to determining who is "in" or "out." This helps the group cohere, and it is sometimes necessitated by damaging secrets that if revealed could lead to the arrest and even death of gang members. Because of this last fact, the expression: "Once in—never out" is the de facto motto of many gangs.

In addition, gang members who live in chronically depressed communities are used to well-meaning individuals like school-based mediators offering short-term help and then disappearing. This serves to increase the distrust they have for outsiders.

School mediators must be cognizant of this dynamic and understand that building trust is a slow process where gangs are concerned. Though mediators should not tolerate inappropriate gang behavior, relationships must be based upon mutual respect. Gang members are more likely to change their behavior when adults believe in them and see them as people first, not only as gang members. Community-based gang specialists are a model here: They are often former gang members themselves who live in the same neighborhood as the gangs with which they work.

Gang-affiliated students are especially likely to feel alienated and uncomfortable in school. Strive to get to know them before one *needs* to know them. After identifying potential gang members, reach out to them whenever possible: say hello in the halls, joke with them in the cafeteria line, etc. Because some gang members associate niceness with weakness, it is sometimes best to be restrained initially. Simple gestures, even if ignored at first, can begin the trust-building process.

YOU CANNOT SHAKE HANDS WITH A CLENCHED FIST.
GOLDA MEIR

Gangs

When introducing the mediation process to gang members, explain the guarantee of confidentiality, and any limits upon it, immediately and forthrightly. Strive to enable gang members to make their own decisions at every turn, including whether to try the process at all. Sometimes this means presenting mediation as an option to these students, and then waiting for them to come back. If and when the mediation process begins, start with extensive private sessions to provide a safe setting in which gang-affiliated youth can openly discuss their concerns.

- **Begin with the needs of the gang members.** Gang members have been told countless times, explicitly as well as implicitly, that what they do is wrong. When involved in a dispute in school, there usually is a great deal of pressure put upon them by the school administration. The problem is always defined by outsiders, never by gang members themselves.

ATTENTION IS A TACIT AND CONTINUED COMPLIMENT.

ANN SOPHIE SWETCHINE

Mediators must be perceived as separate from all this. First and foremost, contradict gang members' expectations and ask: "What do you want? What are your concerns; what do you want to change about the way things are?" This represents such a change for many gang-affiliated students that on its own, it goes a long way towards winning their trust and investment in the process. Issues as defined by school administrators, parents, and the community can be discussed and possibly resolved, but students must perceive mediation to be working in their interests.

Encouraging gang members to mediate does not imply that the school condones their inappropriate, immoral or illegal behavior. As always, mediation efforts should not compromise a school's disciplinary system in any way. Students who break school rules should still receive appropriate and swift consequences. Rather, school mediators and parties ideally work parallel with an effective disciplinary code.

- **Create a safe environment for negotiations.** Gang members will agree to participate and discuss their concerns in mediation only if they feel that it is safe. These students may have suffered physical violence at the hands of other gang members, and their emotions may run high. Experienced mediators clearly demonstrate their control during gang mediations, erring on the side of controlling the process too much (although always respectfully so) rather than too little.

Begin by asking those who know best, gang members themselves, what will make them feel safe. Administrators should be consulted as well. School mediators have taken uncharacteristic measures to ensure the security of gang mediation sessions, including:

—implementing a "no-weapons" policy and frisking each student prior to entering the mediation room

—prohibiting students from wearing gang-related clothing to sessions

—bringing only spokespeople together, never entire groups, because of the volatility of the situation

—stationing security personnel (usually school police) immediately outside of the session or in the session itself[*]

—escorting gang members to "safe zones" after the mediation session.

Endeavor to get the parties' permission before taking any of these measures. Trust is a two-way street. If mediators expect gang members to trust them (and eventually trust each other), mediators may have to demonstrate their trust in these parties. In one case, gang members who had worked hard to honor a truce felt disrespected by administrators' requests that they pass through metal detectors and security checks prior to mediation. After receiving credible promises from the parties that no violence would occur, mediators met with administrators and received permission to go forward without the metal detectors and security guards. During follow-up meetings, gang members stressed that the trust demonstrated by the administration was a crucial factor in the success of their mediation.

Gangs

---

[*] Municipal police can be used if mediators feel it is necessary, but not if their presence makes gang members uncomfortable.

A final consideration regarding safety is the location where sessions are conducted. There is sometimes great concern among parties that they will be harassed by rival gang members. Secure a space that makes this unlikely if not impossible. Sites that are off school grounds sometimes are perceived as more neutral territory.

- **Involve all gang members in the process, especially in the creation of agreements.** Unless all gang members participate in mediation, individual parties may not speak freely or commit to a specific course of action. This issue is complicated by the fact that some gang members may attend different schools or not attend school at all. Mediators strive to have all gang members participate *that attend the school*. They also encourage trusted adults to contact gang members not in school to ensure that they won't have a negative impact upon the process.

If agreements between gangs are to be effective, ideally every member attending school must sign on. Anything less could lead to a disintegration of the agreement. When a few members are unwilling to sign an agreement that is acceptable to many others, encourage those few to raise their concerns with their peers. They may have detected valid issues that the entire group would benefit from discussing. Consider providing each gang with time to talk in private in order to decide how they want to proceed.

Avoid the appearance of pressuring gang members to sign an agreement. If the terms of the agreement are sound, often these young people will eventually sign on. Students who are ready to "settle" can sign interim agreements that prevent the conflict from escalating while gangs discuss the situation. It is in no one's interest for gangs to sign an agreement that will not work. If only a portion of gang members are willing to ratify an agreement, mediators must decide on a case-by-case basis whether it is nevertheless beneficial to create it.

Gangs

The mediation process is far from a solution to the problems related to youth gangs, solutions which are clearly difficult to achieve. Suppression strategies are not particularly effective. Rather, "community wide efforts that help younger kids do better in school and provide older kids with training programs and jobs appear to be most successful."[32] Law enforcement officials, parents, educators, religious leaders and the business community must work collaboratively to address the problem of youth gangs.

If gang-affiliated young people are involved in conflicts at school, however, mediation can help reduce tensions and prevent violence from escalating. When it works, the relief that parties typically experience at the conclusion of a mediation session is all the more astonishing to gang members who may never have conceived of a resolution to their conflict. But there is much more to learn about this application of mediation. Additional cases need to be mediated to provide a broader base of experience. And a great deal more dialogue needs to occur between school-based mediators, community-based gang intervention specialists, and academics who study gangs.

Resources

Books

Gangs: A Handbook for Community Awareness
Rick Landre, Mike Miller and Dee Porter (New York: Facts on File, 1997)

Gang Violence Prevention
Ulric Johnson and William J. Kreidler
Sunburst Communications
101 Castleton Street, PO Box 100
Pleasantville, NY 10570
(800) 431-1934.
Curriculum for grades 7 - 12, includes student handouts

Gangs

Organizations

The National Youth Gang Center
PO Box 12729
Tallahassee, FL 32317
(850) 385-0600
email: nygc@iir.com
Funded by the US Department of Justice, NYGC serves as a resource for "comprehensive, accurate, consistent and timely national information on youth gangs and gang-related crime"

People in your community who are familiar with gangs.
Many police departments now have gang units, and community agencies and educators in your own or in neighboring school districts might be good resources. Gang members, former gang members, and other students can also help.

Checklist
Mediating Conflicts Involving Youth Gangs

IN GENERAL

✓ Work closely with community-based individuals and agencies (217)

✓ Learn about the gangs in the area (218)

✓ Reach out to gang members before you *need* to know them (219)

INTAKE

✓ Strive to have all gang members *that attend the school* participate in the mediation process (222)

✓ Contact gang members not in school either to invite them to participate or to ensure that they won't have a negative impact upon the process (222)

✓ Begin with the needs of the gang members, asking what *they* want (220)

✓ Explain the guarantee of confidentiality, and any limits upon it, immediately and forthrightly (220)

✓ Enable gang members to make their own decisions when possible (220)

✓ Create a safe environment for negotiations: (220)
  • Ask gang members what they need to feel safe
  • Demonstrate trust in gang members so that they will trust you
  • Locate a site that is safe and perceived to be neutral

MEDIATOR SELECTION

✓ Choose skilled mediators, adults as well as experienced and confident students (218)

✓ Consider using community-based mediators, including ex-gang members (218)

DURING THE SESSION

✓ Emphasize the trust-building process (219)

✓ Err on the side of controlling the process too much (although always respectfully so) rather than too little (221)

✓ Enable gang members to make their own decisions when possible (220)

✓ If agreements are being created, strive to have every gang member attending the school sign on (222)

✓ Avoid the appearance of pressuring gang members to sign an agreement (222)

Gangs

10

OTHER CHALLENGES:

INTERPRETERS, RETURNEES, WITNESSES, PREVENTING VIOLENCE, "WALK-OUTS," CANCELLATIONS AND "NO SHOWS"

Mediating Using Interpreters

Language is crucial to mediation. It is the primary vehicle for expression in a process that is essentially people speaking with one another. As such, it is important to conduct mediation sessions in the language with which parties are most comfortable. The reasons for mediating in parties' first language include:

- It demonstrates respect for them.
- Spoken language has subtleties of meaning determined by tone, context, and inflection. Because mediation depends upon accurate communication among parties and between parties and the mediators, it is essential to conduct sessions in the language with which participants have the greatest facility.
- Mediating is stressful in any language. Mediating in a language other than one's native tongue forces parties to work even harder and waste energy on communication mechanics that would be better

directed towards the substance of the discussion.

- Mediation sessions often engender intense emotions for parties. Those who speak more than one language typically will revert to their first language when they become emotional. Conducting mediation in parties' first language is consistent with this natural tendency.

Some parties, perhaps to "not make trouble," consent to mediate in English even when they would be more comfortable in another language. Try to arrange to mediate in their first language nonetheless. If the school has a peer mediation program, the diversity of the mediators should make it possible to mediate in the major languages spoken by the student body. In North American schools, mediation sessions have been successfully conducted in languages from Spanish to Khmer to American Sign Language.

It is not always possible to mediate in parties' native tongues, however. The school may not have access to a mediator that speaks the language in question. Or one mediator may be fluent in this language while the second mediator is not. The parties themselves may even speak different languages and be unable to communicate with each other directly, no less than with the mediators. At these times, mediators count on the assistance of interpreters.

What is an Interpreter?

Although the word "translator" is often used to refer to someone who converts what a person is saying in one language to another, the correct term is "interpreter." Technically, an interpreter works with the spoken word, while a translator works with the written word.

The two major forms of interpreting are known as "simultaneous" and "consecutive." In simultaneous interpretation, the words of the speaker are interpreted as they are spoken, with only the slightest of delays. The most familiar example of simultaneous interpretation is at the United Nations, where a speech in one language is simultaneously interpreted by different highly trained personnel into the dozens of other languages spoken by UN delegates. American Sign Languages interpreters usually work simultaneously as well.

With consecutive interpretation, the speaker talks for a short while and then pauses while their words are interpreted. A minute of speech is followed by a minute of interpretation. Consecutive interpretation is the most common method of interpreting in mediation for one practical reason: Two languages spoken simultaneously in one room quickly become an unintelligible jumble. Unless one has a complex system of microphones and head sets like the United Nations, or the languages in question use differing media as in American Sign Language and spoken English, simultaneous interpretation is unworkable. Consecutive interpretation can also create a more calm and considered atmosphere in mediation sessions because parties are forced to take frequent breaks while speaking.

Who Will Interpret?

When confronted with a dispute that requires interpretation, the first challenge for coordinators and mediators is to locate the interpreter. Because interpreting is a complex skill that adults devote their professional lives to mastering, strive as a first option to work with people who have experience in this role. Some localities have agencies which can provide the names of professional interpreters. In the United States, if parties have a disability that necessitates the assistance of an interpreter, the Americans With Disabilities Act (ADA) *requires* schools to provide an appropriate interpreter.

When using community-based interpreters is not possible, school mediators/coordinators improvise using resources available within their buildings. The "non-professional" interpreting options include:

1. **One of the mediators can act as interpreter.** A mediator can interpret one party's words to another party, or interpret both parties'

words to their co-mediator. Because the combined responsibility of mediating and interpreting is difficult for even the most experienced mediators, it is preferable *not* to use this option.

2. **A trained mediator who is not mediating the case can act as interpreter.** This is better than the first option because the interpreter knows the language and the mediation process, but does not have to do both simultaneously. Some schools have used student trainees who are not yet ready to mediate as interpreters.

3. **An individual based in the school but not connected to the dispute or the mediation effort can act as interpreter.** This works quite well and often results in the interpreter wanting to be trained as a mediator.

4. **A witness or an ally of one of the parties can act as interpreter.** Sometimes there is no choice but to use allies of the parties as interpreters. Although not ideal, such ad hoc "friends of the mediation process" can have a distinctive conciliatory influence upon parties. Allies thrust into the role of interpreter may quickly comprehend the responsibility involved, put aside their partisanship, and work to engender trust and mutual understanding among their peers. One of the unavoidable limitations of this approach is that if private sessions are needed, it is awkward to have the ally of one party interpret the private session of the other.

How to Prepare Interpreters

There are notable similarities between mediating and interpreting. Both roles require that practitioners withhold their personal opinions, and both are bound by ethical obligations that include keeping information discovered during the work confidential. At least in one significant sense, however, the goals of interpreters and mediators are in direct conflict.

Interpreters strive for the highest degree of accuracy in their work. They see themselves as neutral—ideally, next to invisible—transmitters or conduits of the words of others, including the intent and tone of what is expressed by those words. If one party says angrily: "Oliver is a slime-ball because he has been picking on me lately," the interpreter would use the most accurate representation of that sentiment in the second language.

Mediators have a different objective. Although they too place great stock in determining the true meaning of what parties say, the mediator's goal is to help parties work together to resolve their conflict. As such, they allow themselves latitude for the manipulation and filtering of communication. Mediators paraphrase and "re-frame" what parties say to enable them to understand and accept one another. This is especially true for statements that mediators judge to be unnecessarily inflammatory. Mediators might paraphrase the party's comment "Oliver is a slime-ball because he has been picking on me lately" as: "Deana is very concerned because she feels that you have been picking on her lately." They would find it counterproductive and poor practice to convey this statement exactly as it was spoken.

Clearly, a tension exists, and this tension is exacerbated by the fact that parties sometimes make comments in the presence of adversaries who do not understand their language that they would never say otherwise. Because mediation depends upon forthright and faithful communication between the parties, however, interpreters in mediation sessions should maintain a commitment to precision above all else. If they must err, they should err on the side of accuracy rather than take the liberty of altering parties' statements.

When using interpreters, especially non-professional interpreters who are unfamiliar with mediation, it is important to explain their role prior to the session. Be sure to discuss the following:
   —Interpreters represent the mediation program, and they must show the same respect and courtesy to parties as do the mediators.
   —Interpreters must attempt to convey the true meaning of parties' words and beware of the natural tendency to "soften" what parties say.
   —Interpreters must remain neutral conduits of information and guard

against forming opinions of what is being said that would inhibit their work.

—Interpreters, like mediators, must agree to keep all information confidential that they learn during the session. This commitment is of profound importance.

Ensure that parties feel comfortable with the individuals who will serve as interpreters. Parties and mediators should also be apprised of their special responsibilities when interpreters are used. Ask parties to speak slowly, avoid slang and idioms, and pause when they speak to allow for interpretation. Mediators need to be aware of the following:

- Although they might not understand a party's words, mediators should look at the speaking party rather than at the interpreter. It is a common mistake to only look at the interpreter, which not only makes the speaking party feel isolated, but causes mediators to miss essential non-verbal cues.
- Mediators should be prepared for the greater time commitment and frustration that may result from managing the process in more than one language.
- Mediators working with parties who are hearing-impaired should wave to get parties' attention, face the light source, speak slowly, and keep hands and food away from their face.

When everyone understands their role, mediating with interpreters is a fascinating and effective practice.

When Students Return to Mediation Many Times

Sometimes the same student returns to mediation numerous times, whether to discuss a conflict that has already been mediated or to mediate a dispute with a different party. Contrary to many educators' first impressions, this is to be expected and encouraged. Although mediation empowers parties to resolve conflicts on their own, it is unrealistic to expect that after one experience students will never need assistance again. In fact, with only a few exceptions, there should be no limitation on students' access to mediation. The reasons for this include:

- **Conflict is a normal part of life.** Interpersonal conflicts do not cease just because there is a mediation effort in a school, and students who have been to mediation once do not stop having conflicts. When young people cannot resolve a conflict on their own, coming to mediation—once, twice, or twenty times—is exactly what educators should encourage.

- **People learn by repetition and reinforcement.** Schools must expose students to non-violent methods of conflict resolution repeatedly if they expect to counter the negative modeling of the streets, the media, and sometimes even the home. With time, the message does get through. Students who reluctantly come to mediation *after* a fight one semester, seek out mediation services *before* they become involved in a fight the next. Observing such positive behavioral change is one of the greatest satisfactions for those who mediate in schools.

- **People and relationships change.** Even when students create an agreement in good faith, they may need to modify their agreement because of subsequent developments. Actions that seemed realistic and productive during mediation might prove to be unworkable in the real world. And strategies that made sense for the first month might not make sense for the next.

- **New parties learn about mediation.** If a student returns to mediation with different people, it exposes the new parties to the benefits of talking conflicts out instead of fighting them out.

> THERE IS NO WAY TO PEACE...PEACE IS THE WAY.
>
> A. J. MUSTE

Many peer mediation programs even include a clause in every agreement that reads: "If this agreement is not working and we are having problems with each other that we cannot resolve, we agree to come back to mediation."

There *are* circumstances under which educators should deny students access to mediation services, however. These include:

1. **Students do not take the process seriously.** If after fair warning, parties are abusive to mediators or other parties, do not follow the rules of the process, or do not make an honest effort to resolve their dispute, they should not be allowed to mediate. The same holds true on the rare occasions that students fabricate conflicts as a joke, or use the act of going to mediation to skip class or to tease one of their peers.

2. **Students use mediation to meet needs that can be better met in other ways.** Sometimes students return to mediation simply because they like the attention they receive from the program. Such "regulars" use any opportunity to refer themselves to mediation. Coordinators should consider referring these students to peer counseling, peer leadership or related programs, training them to be mediators, or finding other ways that they can be involved with the program.

3. **Students do not have the ability to uphold their agreements.** A very small percentage of students are unable to maintain commitments they make in mediation because of cognitive or emotional disabilities. These students should be referred to school counselors for help. Be advised, however, that the label "special needs" is used so broadly that many students so labeled can capably participate in mediation. Students with special needs have made excellent mediators as well.

Aside from the exceptions noted, encourage students to use mediation as often as they like. One final note: The fact that students come to mediation repeatedly may indicate the need to increase their exposure to conflict resolution and communication skills in other forms (thereby increasing their ability to resolve conflicts on their own). Consider strengthening efforts to offer conflict resolution skill-building lessons throughout the curriculum.

Other Challenges

Handling Witnesses

Mediators generally discourage witnesses—people who are not party to a dispute but who vouch for one disputant's interpretation of events—from participating in mediation sessions. Because mediators do not make determinations about the past or recommendations for the future, witnesses' "testimonies" are largely irrelevant to the process. Witnesses can also have a destructive impact in mediation. Their comments and their mere presence in a session can inhibit the development of trust between parties that is necessary for the process to be effective.

On occasion, it does make sense to have witnesses in a session. Parties might make their participation in the process contingent upon the witnesses' presence, and coordinators may decide that it is better to have a session with a witness than to have no session at all. (As discussed in Chapter 2, involving a witness as a confidence builder or advocate, especially for parties who have been the targets of harassment, is often appropriate.) Mediators may also discover after the session is under way that a person who appeared to be a legitimate party is merely an ally of one of the disputants. Under these circumstances, mediators have no choice but to work with witnesses.

Treat witnesses with the same respect and hold them to the same standards of conduct as the parties. Encourage witnesses to present their perspective in the joint session along with the parties. If their presence appears to be innocuous, allow them to remain in the session for its duration. Some witnesses even turn out to be friends of the conciliation effort, helping to bring parties closer together through their comments and observations.

If, as is more often the case, witnesses turn out to have a negative impact on the process, consider asking them to leave. The direct way to accomplish this is to first confirm with the witness herself that she is not a direct party to the dispute. Then explain to the witness and parties why it is preferable to work only with those who are parties to the dispute. If the parties feel comfortable with the mediators, often they will not object to their allies' departure. If necessary, broach this subject in a private session with the party and his or her witnesses. Thank witnesses for their help before dismissing them.

A second, indirect approach to handling witnesses is to use private sessions and caucuses to leave them literally outside of the room. Mediators take a break, and then call only the true parties back to the session. After parties have resolved key issues on their own, witnesses can be invited to return or, with the parties' permission, sent back to class.

In general, the presence of witnesses in mediation sessions should be discouraged. But if coordinators and mediators are comfortable handling them, they will not cause problems on those occasions when they are present during a session.

Preventing Violence During Mediation Sessions

Thankfully, physical violence rarely occurs during school-based mediation sessions. At every turn, coordinators and mediators work to decrease the likelihood of violence. In the intake interview, disputants who are not ready or willing to mediate are screened out. During the session, the way parties are seated, the timing and manner in which parties address one another, even the order that issues are discussed all minimize the chances of violence.

But the threat of violence is never completely absent in mediation, even if every aspect of the process is carried out to perfection. And no mediator, adult or student, is perfect. The mediation process should accommodate the likelihood that coordinators and mediators will make mistakes. Luckily, each mistake can lead to new insights and strategies that minimize the chances of violence in future sessions. Many of the suggestions that follow were discovered this "hard" way:

1. **Use physical barriers.** If one fears in advance that violence is likely, seat parties with a physical barrier like a table or chairs between

them. Also have parties face the mediators and not their adversaries.

2. **Enforce ground rules.** Train mediators to assertively enforce the ground rules of behavior during sessions. It is fine for parties to vent strong feelings, but if they call each other names or make threatening remarks, mediators should quickly and politely ask them to stop. If they do not stop, end the session. Create additional ground rules such as "parties agree to stay seated" when there is a potential for violence.

3. **Use the best mediators.** Use the most confident mediators for sessions in which feelings run high and parties are prone to violent behavior.

4. **Have an adult nearby.** When using student mediators for potentially violent cases, arrange to have the coordinator or another adult support person in the room during the session. In addition, consider conducting the session near or within a space that is associated with adult control: a teacher's office, the counseling center, even the disciplinarian's office if necessary.

5. **Use short sentences and first names.** When parties are upset and threatening to get out of hand, use short, declarative sentences that include their proper name: "Jim, please sit down" or "Leslie, come with me!" Nothing grabs a person's attention like hearing their name. Create a seating chart when necessary to keep many parties' names accessible.

6. **Develop a "time out" signal with parties.** When parties themselves express concern about violence occurring in the session, develop a signal with them in advance that they can use when they need a break.

7. **Break the process into shorter intervals.** Most mediators give each party a chance to tell their complete version of events at the start of a session. But when flaring tempers make it hard for parties to wait their turn, consider asking them to say their stories in short, alternating intervals. Kris gets to speak for three minutes, then Allison does the same, then Kris speaks again, etc. The length of the intervals can grow as parties relax.

Other Challenges

8. **Don't hesitate to stop the process.** Teach mediators to trust their instincts and watch body language and other non-verbal cues (facial expression and color, hand movements, etc.). If they begin to feel uncomfortable and fear an outbreak of violence, they should not hesitate to take a break and escort one of the parties out of the room. Once parties are separated, consult with a coordinator, with co-mediators, and with the parties themselves to determine whether to continue in joint session, move to private sessions, reschedule, or cancel the session altogether.

9. **Balance private and joint sessions.** Although private sessions can be essential when parties have difficulty being in the same room together, try to keep parties in joint session as long as it is helpful. Otherwise, they miss the potentially transformative experience of hearing their adversary's version of events.

10. **Pay attention to parties' fatigue.** When parties are tired and frustrated, they are more likely to act on impulse. Make sure that mediation sessions do not last longer than necessary. Although this is often not an issue—student versus student sessions in middle and high schools average less than one hour—large group and complex interpersonal mediations can run much longer. It is better to schedule an additional meeting than to push parties beyond their limit, even if they themselves want to continue.

11. **Schedule separate sessions for discrete interpersonal conflicts.** When mediators uncover two-party conflicts within a large group dispute, schedule a separate session for each interpersonal dispute. Send students back to class for the interim. One fight occurred when a couple of student parties had to wait in an anteroom for many hours while their friends' conflict was mediated first.

12. **Escort parties back to class.** When parties are unable to reach an agreement during the session, personally escort them back to class (or to the office) if one is concerned that they might fight.

A single violent incident during mediation can be extremely harmful to mediation's reputation within a school. By taking the above precautions, mediators will maintain the field's outstanding record of safe and non-violent sessions.

When Parties Walk Out During a Session

Occasionally, parties will walk out during the middle of a mediation session. Often they do not give warning or ask the mediators' permission; they just stand up and leave the room. This can be disconcerting to mediators who, unless they have been through this before, do not know what to do. It is therefore important to prepare for this contingency.

When parties leave during a mediation session, it is almost always because they are overcome with feeling: anger, sadness, frustration, or embarrassment. They might be on the verge of crying and do not want to do so in front of the other party. They might be so angry that they fear they will become violent if they stay in the room. They might have reached the limit of their frustration. Leaving the session is an instinctive, spontaneous reaction to help them regain control.

Walking out of a session is not necessarily a sign that parties are uninterested in resolving their conflict. If anything, leaving usually indicates the emotional investment that a party *has* made in the process. Although they might not realize it in the moment, it is often in that party's best interest to return to the mediation session. It is also in the school's best interest, as it would be irresponsible to let a party leave a session so upset. If possible, parties who want to end a session should do so only after collecting themselves and carefully considering the ramifications of their decision.

If a party walks out of a mediation session, then, either the coordinator or one of the mediators should immediately follow. Walk with them for a while—moving helps the individual expend emotional energy and gain

Other Challenges

composure. Eventually, guide the party into as safe and private an area as possible (an empty classroom, stairwell, bathroom, corner, etc.). Stand at an angle to them so as to not appear confrontational. Don't push the party to talk initially; just stand with them while they collect themselves.

When they seem ready, try to get the party to communicate. Show concern by asking supportive questions and repeating back their concerns. Once they open up, ask if they would be willing to continue the mediation process. Highlight any progress that has been made during the session, and explain that if they return, the mediators can meet with them alone in a private session.

If approached with sensitivity, most parties will eventually return to participate in the session. When they do, mediators should take special care to minimize their embarrassment and help them "save face." All parties tend to be more attentive after one has walked out, however, and so this can inadvertently move the process forward. In those instances when parties are unwilling to return, their wishes should be respected. Refer them to any other program or individual that might be of help, escort them to wherever they need to go, and treat the case like any other in which no agreement is reached.

One final note: A party walking out of the session can indicate that mediators are not calling for private sessions when necessary. Among the benefits associated with them, private sessions enable parties to stay in the process when it is difficult to speak directly with their adversary. Be sure to consider whether this is the case.

Cancellations and "No Shows"

An unfortunate part of every school mediator's work is parties not showing up for their sessions or canceling them at the last minute. Besides being disappointing for expectant mediators, it is frustrating for coordinators who often invest a good deal of time and energy into scheduling a session. The three most common reasons why parties do not follow through with mediation are:

1. They have been able to resolve the conflict on their own.
2. They honestly forget about the session.
3. They get nervous and decide not to attend the session.

Coordinators and mediators should applaud if parties are able to resolve their differences on their own. More often than not, however, it is one or both of the other factors—fear and forgetfulness—that account for parties not participating in their scheduled session.

Take the following steps to minimize the likelihood of cancellations and no-shows:

- Create an efficient scheduling system so that sessions can be conducted soon after a referral is received. Apart from a requisite "cooling off" period, the shorter the delay between the initial referral and the session, the greater the chances that parties will make it to the session.
- Clarify during the intake interview whether parties are committed to using mediation. If coordinators doubt parties' commitment, confront them about this directly: "You seem to be hesitant about mediation. I think participation in the process could be very helpful, but it is up to you. Are you sure you want to try it?"
- Make sure that the time chosen for the session is acceptable to the parties. When the parties are students, coordinators may need to review their schedule in detail, including when they are having tests, when the football team is playing a game, etc.
- Many young people exemplify the "one day at a time" approach to life; it is therefore necessary to remind them about mediation sessions *on the day they are to be held*. This holds true even if coordinators spoke with them the day before! Reminders should ideally be a standard procedure of school-based mediation efforts. Coordinators

can seek students out, use written reminders, ask homeroom teachers to notify parties, or have student mediators (those mediating the dispute or others) visit the parties.

Despite these preventive measures, eleventh hour cancellations and no shows will still occur. Most coordinators do attempt to contact parties and try again, but that is ultimately an individual decision. Important considerations include the suitability of the case for mediation, the level of interest of the parties, and the expectations of the individual who referred the dispute.

When one party shows up for the session while the other doesn't, meet with this student individually. After introductory remarks, mediators can approach the meeting as they would a private session. Sometimes by simply talking to mediators, a party discovers actions he or she can take unilaterally that will improve the situation. Mediators might also be able to refer the party to other programs that will be of help.

Resources
Books
Interpreting For International Conferences: Problems of Language and Communication
Danica Seleskovitch (Pen and Booth, 1994).
Can be ordered through Registry of Interpreters for the Deaf

Organizations
Registry of Interpreters for the Deaf
8630 Fenton Street, Suite 324
Silver Springs, MD 20910
(301) 608-0050
web site: www.rid.org

There is currently no national or international organization that helps individuals find an interpreter (other than an American Sign

Other Challenges

Language interpreter) in their area. Some places to look for an interpreter include:

- Yellow Pages, under "translators" and "interpreters"
- Schools that teach languages
- Community organizations that serve individuals who speak the languages in question

Checklist
OTHER CHALLENGES

MEDIATING USING INTERPRETERS
✓ Strive to use professional interpreters when possible (229)

✓ School-based interpreting options include: (229)
- One of the mediators
- A trained mediator who is not mediating the case
- An individual based in the school but not connected to the dispute or the mediation effort
- A witness or an ally of one of the parties

✓ Prepare interpreters by reminding them of their responsibility to: (231)
- Show the same respect and courtesy to parties as do the mediators
- Convey the true meaning of parties' words (and beware of the natural tendency to "soften" what parties say)
- Remain neutral conduits of information and ensure that their personal opinions about what parties say does not influence their performance
- Keep all information confidential that they learn during the session

✓ Prepare parties by asking them to: (232)
- Talk slowly
- Avoid slang and idioms
- Pause when speaking to allow time for interpretation

During the session: (232)
✓ Look at the speaking party more than at the interpreter

✓ Prepare for the greater time commitment and frustration that can result from managing the process in more than one language

✓ When working with parties who are hearing-impaired, wave to get parties' attention, face the light source, speak slowly, and keep hands and food away from the face

WHEN STUDENTS RETURN TO MEDIATION MANY TIMES
✓ Encourage parties to come to mediation—once, twice, or twenty times—when they cannot resolve a conflict on their own (233)

✓ The only exceptions are: (234)
- Students who do not take the process seriously
- Students who use mediation to meet needs that can be better met in other ways
- Students who do not have the ability to uphold their agreements

HANDLING WITNESSES

✓ In general, discourage witnesses—people who are not party to a dispute—from participating in mediation sessions (235)

✓ When mediators have no choice but to work with witnesses: (235)
- Treat witnesses with the same respect and hold them to the same standards of conduct as the parties
- Provide witnesses with the opportunity to present their perspective during the joint session

✓ If witnesses have a negative impact on the process, ask them to leave by either: (235)
- Confirming with the witness that he or she is not a direct party to the dispute, explaining why it is preferable to work only with those who are parties to a dispute, and asking them to leave
- Calling for private sessions and then asking only the true parties back to the session

PREVENTING VIOLENCE DURING MEDIATION SESSIONS

✓ Use physical barriers (236)

✓ Enforce ground rules (237)

✓ Use the best mediators (237)

✓ When students are mediating, have an adult nearby (237)

✓ Use short sentences and first names (237)

✓ Develop a "time out" signal with parties (237)

✓ Break the process into shorter intervals (237)

✓ Don't hesitate to end the session (238)

✓ Balance private and joint sessions (238)

✓ Pay attention to parties' fatigue (238)

Other Challenges

✓ Escort parties to class at the conclusion of mediation sessions (238)

✓ For group disputes, schedule separate sessions for discrete interpersonal conflicts (238)

WHEN PARTIES WALK OUT DURING A SESSION

✓ Immediately follow and walk with the party (239)

✓ Guide the party into as safe and private an area as possible (240)

✓ Stand at an angle so as to not appear confrontational

✓ Don't push the party to talk; wait until they seem ready

✓ Show concern by asking supportive questions and repeating back the party's concerns

✓ Highlight any progress that has been made during the session

✓ Explain that mediators can meet with the party alone in a private session

✓ Ask if the party would be willing to continue the mediation process

✓ If the party does return, take special care to minimize his or her embarrassment

✓ If the party is unwilling to return, refer him or her to any other program or individual that might be of help and escort the party to wherever they need to go

✓ If parties walk out often, consider: Are mediators calling for private sessions when necessary?

CANCELLATIONS AND "NO SHOWS"

✓ Prevent cancellations and "no shows" by: (240)

- Creating an efficient scheduling system that enables sessions to be conducted soon after a referral is received

- Clarifying during the intake interview whether parties are committed to using mediation

- Ensuring that the time chosen for the session is acceptable to the parties

- Reminding parties about mediation sessions *on the day they are to be held*

I AM DONE WITH GREAT THINGS
AND BIG THINGS, GREAT
INSTITUTIONS AND BIG
SUCCESSES, AND I AM FOR
THOSE TINY INVISIBLE MOLECULAR
MORAL FORCES THAT WORK FROM
INDIVIDUAL TO INDIVIDUAL,
CREEPING THROUGH THE
CRANNIES OF THE WORLD LIKE SO
MANY ROOTLETS, OR LIKE THE
CAPILLARY OOZING OF WATER,
YET WHICH, IF YOU GIVE THEM
TIME, WILL REND THE HARDEST
MONUMENTS OF MAN'S PRIDE.

WILLIAM JAMES

Notes

1 Bush and Folger, *The Promise of Mediation* (San Francisco: Jossey Bass, 1994).

2 *The American Heritage Dictionary*. (Boston: Houghton Mifflin Company, 1975).

3 *The American Heritage Dictionary*. (Boston: Houghton Mifflin Company, 1975).

4 Howard Gadlin, "Careful Maneuvers: Mediating Sexual Harassment," *Negotiation Journal* 7 (1991): 139-153.

5 See *Students Resolving Conflict*, pages 92 to 95 for more information about how the mediation and disciplinary systems in a school can work together most effectively.

6 Marty Price, "Can Mediation Produce Justice? A Discussion for Mediators and Others," (Unpublished paper), p. 4.

7 See *Students Resolving Conflict*, pages 130 to 135, for more information about conducting intake interviews.

8 See *Students Resolving Conflict*, pages 96 to 99, for more information about confidentiality in peer mediation programs.

9 Nan Stein, Nancy Marshall and Linda Tropp, *Secrets in Public: Sexual Harassment in Our Schools* (Wellesley, MA: Wellesley College Center for Research on Women, 1993) Excerpted in Seventeen magazine.

10 85% of females and 76% of males reported at least one incident.

11 *"Hostile Hallways: The AAUW Survey on Sexual Harassment in America's Schools,"* (Conducted by Louis Harris and Associates, June 1993). Sixteen hundred public school students—male and female, grades 8 and 11—were surveyed.

12 *Hostile Hallways.*

13 Two-thirds of the over 4,000 girls who responded to the Wellesley study said that their harassment happened in public, where other students witnessed it.

14 *Sexual Harassment Guidance: Peer Harassment*, Draft policy (The United States Department of Education, Office for Civil Rights, August, 1996).

15 Gadlin, p. 141.

16 USED/OCR, p. 8.

17 See *Students Resolving Conflict*, pages 238-243, for more information on the legal implications of operating school-based peer mediation programs.

[18] Gadlin, p. 148.

[19] *Sexual Harassment in the Schools: Legal Resource Kit* (New York: NOW Legal Defense and Education Fund, 1995) p. 4.

[20] *Statistical Abstract of the United States*, Washington, D.C. : U.S. Bureau of the Census, 1992: and Kinsey's estimates

[21] Singer, Bennett and Dechamps, David. *Gay and Lesbian Stats: A Pocket Guide of Facts and Figures* (NY: The New Press, 1994).

[22] Massachusetts Governor's Commission on Gay and Lesbian Youth, 1993.

[23] From the American Association of the University Women study conducted by Louis Harris and Associates.

[24] Singer and Dechamps.

[25] *Fact File: Lesbian, Gay, and Bisexual Youth*, (Hetrick-Martin Institute, 1992).

[26] Gary Remafedi, "Adolescent Homosexuality." *Pediatrics* 79 (1987) and *Fact File: Lesbian, Gay, and Bisexual Youth.*

[27] US Department of Health and Human Services, *Report of the Secretary's Task Force on Youth Suicide*, 1989.

[28] Merry, S. and Rocheleau, A., *Mediation in Families: A Study of the Children's Hearings Project*, 1985.

[29] See *Students Resolving Conflict* for more information on conducting intake interviews, pages 130 to 135.

[30] Spergel, Irving, et. al, *Gang Suppression and Intervention: Community Models* (Research Summary), Office of Juvenile Justice and Delinquency Prevention, US Department of Justice, Washington DC, 1994, p. 1.

[31] Howell, James C., Gangs, Office of Juvenile Justice and Delinquency Prevention, *Fact Sheet #12*, 1994, p. 1.

[32] Irving Spergel, professor of Sociology at University of Chicago, and gang researcher, quoted in Howell, *Gangs*, p. 2.

Bibliography

Bryant, Anne L. "Hostile Hallways: The AAUW Survey on Sexual Harassment in America's Schools." *Journal of School Health* vol. 63 (October 1993): 355.

Bush, Baruch and Folger, Joseph. *The Promise of Mediation: Responding to Conflict Through Empowerment and Recognition.* San Francisco: Jossey Bass, 1994.

Butterfield, George. "To Mediate or Not to Mediate?" *School Safety* (Fall 1994): 15-17.

Center for Restorative Justice and Mediation. *Victim Offender Mediation Training Manual.* School of Social Work, University of Minnesota, 1996.

Coleman, Peter and Deutsch, Morton. "The Mediation of Interethnic Conflict in Schools." p. 371-395 in *Toward A Common Destiny: Improving Race and Ethnic Relations in America*, edited by Hawley and Jackson. San Francisco: Jossey-Bass, 1995.

Compton, Randy and Paterson, Maia. *Peer Mediation in Action (Implementation Guide).* Niles IL: United Learning, 1997.

D'Andrea, Michael and Daniels, Judy. "Promoting Peace in Our Schools: Developmental, Preventive and Multicultural Considerations." *The School Counselor* vol. 44 (September 1996): 59-63.

Davis, Albie M. and Salem, Richard A. "Dealing with Power Imbalances in the Mediation of Interpersonal Disputes." *Mediation Quarterly* no. 6 (December 1984).

Fleming, Thomas W. and Moriarty, Anthony. "Youth Gangs Aren't Just A Big City Problem Anymore." *The Executive Educator* (July 1990): 13-16.

Gadlin, Howard. "Careful Maneuvers: Mediating Sexual Harassment." *Negotiation Journal* vol. 7, no. 2 (April 1991): 139-153.

Gay and Lesbian Defenders and Advocates. *Guide to Student Rights and Resources in Massachusetts Elementary and Secondary Schools.* Boston: Park Square Advocates.

Gay and Lesbian Defenders and Advocates. *The Legal Rights of Public School Students and Teachers.* Boston: Park Square Advocates.

Goldstein, Susan B. "Cultural Issues in Community Mediation" in *Conflict Analysis and Resolution as Education.* Washington: National Institute for Dispute Resolution.

Goodwin, Megan P., Roscoe, Bruce and Strouse, Jeremiah S. "Sexual Harassment: Early Adolescents' Self Reports of Experiences and Acceptance." *Adolescence* (Fall 1994): 515.

Greenhouse, Linda. "Court Opens Path for Student Suits in Sex-Bias Cases," *New York Times* 27 February 1992, sec. A, p. 1.

Guzman, Dan (Community Youth Gang Services Project, Los Angeles, California). Conversation with author, 2 August 1996.

Howell, James C. *Gangs* (Fact Sheet #12). Office of Juvenile Justice and Delinquency Prevention (April 1994): 1.

Keeney Sara, and Smith, Melinda. "Mediating Gang Conflicts in Schools" *The Fourth R* vol. 62: 7.

Kohls, L. Robert. *Developing Intercultural Awareness*. Washington: The Society for Intercultural Education, Training and Research, 1981.

Landre, Rick, Miller, Mike and Porter, Dee. *Gangs: A Handbook for Community Awareness*. New York: Facts on File, 1997.

LeBaron Duryea, Michelle. "Key Findings of Community Research and Literature Review" in *Conflict Analysis and Resolution as Education*. Washington: National Institute for Dispute Resolution.

Levine, Naomi Z. "Challenges of Sexual Harassment Mediation on Campus." *The Fourth R* vol. 79: 19-21.

Menkin, Elizabeth, "Life After Death," *San Jose Mercury News*, 4 September 1994.

Moore, Christopher. "Have Process, Will Travel: Reflections on Democratic Decision Making and Conflict Management Practice Abroad." *NIDR Forum* (Winter 1993): 6-9.

National School Safety Center. *Gangs in Schools: Breaking Up Is Hard to Do* (California: Pepperdine University Press, 1988).

NOW Legal Defense and Education Fund. *Sexual Harassment in the Schools: Legal Resource Kit*.

NOW Legal Defense and Education Fund. *Fact Sheet on Sexual Harassment Legal Standards Under Title IX*.

Orell, Linda Henry and Tabish, Kenneth R. "Respect: Gang Mediation at Albuquerque, New Mexico's Washington Middle School." *The School Counselor* vol. 44 (September 1996): 65-70.

Price, Marty. "Can Mediation Produce Justice?: A Discussion for Mediators and Others." Unpublished Paper.

Price, Marty. "Comparing Victim Offender Mediation Program Models." *Victim Offender Mediation* vol. 6, no. 1 (Summer 1995).

Seleskovitch, Danica. *Interpreting for International Conferences: Problems of Language and Communication*. Pen and Booth, 1994.

Short, James F. Jr. *Gangs and Adolescent Violence*. (Paper published by the Center for the Study and Prevention of Violence, University of Colorado, Boulder, June 1996).

Sisson, V. Shamin, and Todd, Sybil R. "Using Mediation in Response to Sexual Assault on College and University Campuses." *NASPA Journal* vol.

32, no. 4 (Summer 1995): 262-269.

Sorti, Craig. *The Art of Crossing Cultures*. Maine: Intercultural Press, 1989.

Spergel, Irving, et. al. "Gang Suppression and Intervention: Community Models (Research Summary)." Washington: Office of Juvenile Justice and Delinquency Prevention, 1994.

Stamato, Linda. "Sexual Harassment in the Workplace: Is Mediation an Appropriate Forum?" *Mediation Quarterly* vol. 10, no 2 (Winter 1992): 167-172.

State of California Department of Youth Authority. *Gang Violence Reduction Project: Fourth Evaluation Report, July 1979-June 1980* (January 1981).

Susskind, Lawrence and Jeffrey, Cruikshank. *Breaking the Impasse: Consensual Approaches to Resolving Public Disputes*. New York: Basic Books, 1987.

"The Case of the I-205 Rock Throwers," flyer from the Victim Offender Reconciliation Program, Portland, Oregon.

The Minnesota Department of Children, Families and Learning. *Respecting Everyone's Ability to Resolve Problems: Restorative Measures*. (August 1996).

Umbreit, Mark S. "A Humanistic Mediation Model: Moving to A Higher Plane." *VOMA Quarterly* vol. 7, no. 3 (Fall/Winter 1996).

Umbreit, Mark S., and Niemeyer, Mike. "Victim Offender Mediation: From the Margins to the Mainstream." *Perspectives* (Summer 1996).

US Department of Education, Office for Civil Rights. "Sexual Harassment Guidance: Harassment of Students by School Employees, Other Students, or Third Parties; Notice." *Federal Register* vol. 62, no. 49, part VII (13 March 1997): 12034-12051.

US Department of Education, Office for Civil Rights. *Sexual Harassment Guidance: Peer Harassment*. Draft Policy (August, 1996).

US Department of Justice, Office of Juvenile Justice and Delinquency Prevention. 1995 *National Youth Gang Survey: Program Summary*. August 1997.

Wahrhaftig, Paul. "Norming, Storming and Forming a Gang Related Model for Conflict Resolution." *Conflict Resolution Notes* vol. 15, nos. 1 and 2 (September 1997): 8-10.

Weddle, C.J. "The Case For Structured Negotiation In Sexual Misconduct Cases" *Synthesis: Law and Policy in Higher Education* vol. 4 (1992): 291-292.

West, Cornel. "Learning to Talk of Race" *New York Times* Magazine, 2 August 1992, p. 24-26.

About School Mediation Associates

Founded in 1984, School Mediation Associates (SMA) became the first organization devoted to the application and promotion of mediation in the schools. Since then, many thousands of educators, students, and parents have participated in SMA training programs around the world, and thousands more use SMA materials in their schools.

School Mediation Associates offers a range of awareness and skill building training programs on mediation, negotiation, communication, violence prevention, and prejudice reduction. SMA pays special attention to the issue of institutional change and strives to create programs with longevity. SMA also places primary importance upon conducting culturally relevant training programs.

Goals of SMA Training Programs:
- To teach students and educators the skills necessary to resolve conflict non-violently and collaboratively.
- To teach an approach to problem solving that welcomes diversity and respects difference of opinion.
- To help students and educators see conflict as an opportunity for personal and institutional growth.
- To provide educators with the knowledge, the experience and the materials necessary to conduct their own mediation/conflict resolution trainings, and integrate conflict resolution into their professional practice and curricula.
- To transform schools into safer, more caring, and more effective institutions.

In addition to providing training, SMA staff mediators also regularly mediate complex disputes that occur in schools.

For more information, contact us at:

School Mediation Associates
134-B Standish Road, Watertown, MA 02472 USA
(617) 926-5969/web site: www.schoolmediation.com

Order Form

Fax Orders: (617) 926-5969
Toll-free Telephone Orders: (800) 833-3318
Postal Orders: SMA, 134-B Standish Road, Watertown, MA, 02472, USA
Web Site: www.schoolmediation.com

PLEASE SEND:

_____ copies of **The School Mediator's Field Guide** at
$24.95 per copy   _____

_____ copies of **Students Resolving Conflict** at $14.95 per
copy   _____

_____ Information about School Mediation Associates   __Free__

                                       SUBTOTAL: _____

SALES TAX: Please add 5% for books shipped to
Massachusetts addresses   _____

SHIPPING: $4.50 for first book and $2.50 for each
additional book   _____

                                       TOTAL: _____

PAYMENT (check one):

___ Check enclosed

___ Bill my school (must include PO #) PO #:

___ Mastercard/Visa (circle one)   Credit Card #:

Expiration Date: Cardholder's Signature: _____

Name (please print):
School Name:
Address (home or school):
City: State: Zip:
Telephone: Fax:

Call toll free and order now!
(800) 833-3318